THE COMPLETELY
USELESS
UNAUTHORISED
STAR TREK
ENCYCLOPEDIA

THE COMPLETELY USELESS UNAUTHORISED *STAR TREK* ENCYCLOPEDIA

Chris Howarth and Steve Lyons

First published in Great Britain in 1997 by
Virgin Publishing Ltd
332 Ladbroke Grove
London W10 5AH

ISBN 0 7535 0198 8

Typeset by Galleon Typesetting, Ipswich
Printed and bound in Great Britain by
Mackays of Chatham PLC

CONTENTS

Dedicated to Paul Simpson (Dreamwatch) and Anthony Brown (SFX), who both promised good reviews if we gave them a mention. Also, to John, Gary and the gang at Titan's Star Trek Monthly (a snip at £3.15), in case they're equally corrupt.

ABOUT THIS BOOK

First of all, we should make something clear. In our last book of this kind, *Doctor Who – The Completely Useless Encyclopedia*, we may have inadvertently given the impression that we thought *Star Trek* was crap. However, nothing could be further from the truth. We love it – well, apart from *Voyager* and the odd-numbered movies, obviously. We watch every episode, we picked up a good half-dozen issues of *The Official Star Trek Fact Files* before we worked out how much the set would cost, one of us admits to a schoolboy crush on Janice Rand and the other still has some World Distributors annuals. So, all in all, we're delighted to have this opportunity to make a bit of cash off the back of the series. And, hopefully, the fact that we've had to approach the work from a UK perspective (what with living there and all) won't preclude it from achieving Pocket Book-sized sales. Not that this was our idea, you understand. Despite the fact that neither of us is an overweight female who feels no shame when dressed in a skin-tight Starfleet uniform, Virgin approached us to do this follow-up volume even before the *Doctor Who* book went on sale (that's how good it is, so rush out and buy it now). We were slightly reticent at first, not knowing how devoted Trekkies might react to our lampooning their idols. However, we soon realised we'd be able to out-run most of them anyway, and decided to go for it. We still had some doubts about the ethics of writing a factual tome when we didn't know much about the subject concerned, but Virgin swiftly reassured us on this score by publishing *The New Trek Programme Guide* (we almost wish we'd gone for the New Trek tag ourselves, just to see how the sales department abbreviated *The Completely Useless New*

Trek Encyclopedia in their literature). And so, we found ourselves with the arduous task of researching a cultural phenomenon, an exemplary metaphor for the human condition that provided a beacon of hope for a Utopian future. Or, as we've fondly come to think of it, an American TV show. We spent literally hours perusing the exploits of Kirk and Spock and their Starfleet colleagues (or *Kirk* and *Spock* and their *Starfleet* colleagues, as *Star Trek Monthly* would have it). We pored over books and magazines, checked out postings on the internet and even thought about attending a convention, but didn't quite make it. We didn't get around to reading the novels either. We originally wanted to sub-title this book 'Everything you need to know about *Star Trek*', but our manuscript was returned on the basis that it was only two pages long. Fortunately, the flexible encyclopedia format allows us to eschew such unimportant facts as episode guides, production details, behind-the-scenes trivia, etc., and just include the amusing and bizarre stuff that we think you'll enjoy (or, put another way, we wrote what we felt like). If you're after a detailed history of *Star Trek* in all its incarnations, then check out one of those ten million or so works that purport to comprise one. If you're an ardent fan who knows everything about the series anyway but still has to buy anything with the words 'Star' and 'Trek' on it, then give us your cash. And if you're not a fan at all, but don't mind watching *Star Trek* and laughing at those people who take it all too seriously, then you can give us your cash too.

Steve Lyons and Chris Howarth,
The planet Vulcan
(but the one from *Doctor Who*), 1997

THE OBLIGATORY *STAR TREK* EPISODE GUIDE

Season One (1973–74)
Yesteryear, One of our Planets is Missing, The Lorelei Signal, More Tribbles, More Troubles, The Survivor, The Infinite Vulcan, The Magic of Megas-Tu, Once Upon a Planet, Mudd's Passion, The Terratin Incident, Time Trap, The Ambergris Element, Slaver Weapon, Beyond the Farthest Star, The Eye of the Beholder, Jihad

Season Two (1974–75)
The Pirates of Orion, BEM, Practical Joker, Albatross, How Sharper than a Serpent's Tooth, The Counter-Clock Incident

A number of live-action *Star Trek* episodes were also produced.

A

ADMIRAL: Mysterious, unnamed character from the pilot episode of *The Next Generation*. He just happened to be played by DeForest Kelley, star of *The Original Series*, and was about the same age as, oh, as Doctor McCoy would be, we suppose. He had apparently retired from the medical division of Starfleet and he hinted at a dislike of transporters and a relationship of some sort with a ship named *Enterprise*. Hmm, wonder who that could have been, then? Not our Doctor Leonard McCoy, obviously, else surely they'd have come clean and made no Bones about it.

ALERT SIRENS: There were many great technological advances in the years between the original five-year mission and that of *The Next Generation*. But, by the sound of things, Starfleet still had a load of old emergency alarms in stock that needed using up.

'ALL-NEW ADVENTURES OF THE USS *ENTERPRISE* AND ITS CREW': What US publishers Ballantine boasted in the cover blurbs for their series of ten *Star Trek Logs* by noted SF writer Alan Dean Foster (reprinted in the UK by Corgi and again in the US by Pocket Books – in fact, they've been printed by just about everyone). Not an entirely justified claim, as the adventures in question were a bit similar, nay identical, to those seen in *The Animated Series*. So unconvincing were Ballantine that they even admitted to the stories' derivative roots elsewhere on their covers. Perhaps they were just confused by Gene Roddenberry's persistent denial of *TAS*'s existence.

ANBO-JYTSU: Described by Kyle Riker as 'the ultimate evolution in the martial arts'. Odd that, because it actually looked like a cross between *Gladiators* and *Mighty Morphin' Power Rangers*.

ANDORIANS: Trend-setting race of blue-skinned aliens, whose antennaed appearance doubtless inspired the deely-bopper craze of the '70s.

ANDRECE, ALYCE: Talented actress though she was, she was only able to handle 250 roles in 'I, Mudd'. Fortunately, her twin sister Rhae was equally talented and able to play Alyce No. 251 through to 500. This inspired casting was especially convenient when the director required more than one of the supposedly identical androids to appear in the same scene. Now, if only the actresses' parents had had triplets . . .

***ANIMATED SERIES, THE*:** Award-winning follow up to *The Original Series*, which featured many of the creative talents behind its forerunner. Virtually all of the original cast* were hired to reprise their roles, and many other characters and concepts from the live-action version were revisited: Roger C Carmel returned as Harry Mudd, Stanley Adams reprised Cyrano Jones, Mark Lenard made the second of his many appearances as Sarek, while his wife Amanda was played by, erm, Majel Barrett. These two seasons should have been the ideal conclusion to the *Enterprise*'s curtailed five-year mission. Yet, for some reason we cannot fathom, Gene Roddenberry refused to accept the cartoons as canonical. OK, so *The Barely Animated Series* would have made a more appropriate sub-title and, granted, most of the aliens sounded like James Doohan and, admittedly, it was sometimes a little obvious (the Aquans were aquatic, the Avian bird-like and the Felinoid M'Ress was from the planet Cait in the Lynx system). But apart from that . . .

* *Walter Koenig being the exception, though he did write one of them. We were tempted to make a joke about the cartoon's producers thinking he was better at writing than at doing a Russian accent, but, having been brought up in a Russian household, Koenig's accent is authentic. Bugger.*

ANTIQUE VEHICLES: What a stroke of luck that this is one of Tom Paris's hobbies, else the crew of *Voyager* might have been a bit confused when they encountered that 1936 Ford truck floating in space on the other side of the galaxy (in 'The 37s'). And what about Janeway, eh? Not to be outdone, she immediately revealed the hitherto unsuspected talent of being able to identify an animal from one sniff of the merest calcified residue of its dung. Blimey, with a multi-skilled crew like that, it's a wonder they aren't home yet.

ANYA: A pre-Odo shape-shifter. She could do young babe, old boiler, bug-eyed furry midget and bug-eyed furry tall bloke. In the latter form, she had a bit of a one-sided set-to with Worf. He waited until she had turned into an old woman again before deciding to fight back.

APOLLO COMMAND MODULE: Along with a couple of diddy astronauts, this spacecraft came out in the *Star Trek Inner Space* series. All right, so it's a spaceship, and a bloke called Apollo was in *The Original Series*, but it was still rather a strange choice for inclusion. For one thing, we can't see it being much use against the Romulan Warbird included in the set. Still, with all those never-heard-from-again space vessels that NASA inadvertently provided for *Star Trek* plots, perhaps a reciprocal deal was only fair.

'APPLE, THE': Despite its exploding rocks and projectile-firing flowers, it was evident that this *TOS* episode was a Garden of Eden style biblical allegory. So there was really no need for Kirk, Spock and McCoy to labour the point during the jokey epilogue. No need for that big papier-mâché serpentine rock either.

APRIL, ROBERT T: The name of the captain in Gene Roddenberry's earliest *Star Trek* drafts. Simply because of this, it has since been established in the official *Star Trek* time-lines that April was indeed the *Enterprise*'s first captain. Naturally, however, it took the imaginative *Animated Series* to give substance to the character.

ARCHAEOLOGY: A favourite hobby of Jean-Luc Picard, though you'd have thought that scrabbling about in the dirt looking for traces of long-buried civilisations would have lost some of its appeal following the discovery of time travel.

AREX: Gangling great orange-skinned alien who, for reasons best known to Filmation, replaced Chekov as the ensign in *The Animated Series*. Arex was an Edoan, which meant he had three arms and three legs, making him ideally suited to the cartoon world. Although he hardly ever lifted a tentacle, the impact of the character was such that he was picked up by DC for a run in one of their many *Star Trek* comic books. Then along came Paramount, who insisted on the removal of this 'unofficial' character. Bastards.

***ARIES*, USS:** Rubbish ship and just one of loads of which Will Riker was offered the command. Picard, obviously keen to see the back of him, advised his Number One to take the job and claimed that the *Aries* would soon be 'vibrant with his authority, style and vision'. We suspect he was taking the piss.

<hr>

TEN OTHER FEDERATION STARSHIPS

1: USS *Yorktown*. This was the name by which the *Enterprise* was almost known. Dull or what? A ship of the same name almost turned up in *TOS* – the *Enterprise* was supposed to rendezvous with it, but got delayed and probably didn't bother.

2: *Defiant*. Hard ship introduced into *DS9* to make it more like proper *Trek*. Usually this ship can't take off without practically the entire crew of the station jumping on board – even if they're doing so at the risk of facing a court martial, or they're eighty years old or something. Yet in *First Contact*, Worf's is the only familiar face on it. Odd, huh?

3: *Enterprise E.* Starship commissioned (predictably) in time for *First Contact*, and ideal for marketing in toy form – as are its crew in their snazzy new Starfleet uniforms, the *Phoenix*, the Borg, the supporting characters . . .

4: *Constellation.* Funny how most Federation starships in *TOS* looked like the *Enterprise* (yeah, we know, Constitution Class). What may have made practical sense at the time must now seem like a missed opportunity – with a little foresight there could have been at least another box worth of micro-machines. (See also USS *EXCALIBUR*, USS *EXETER*, USS *HOOD*, USS *LEXINGTON* and USS *POTEMKIN*; and make that two more boxes of micro-machines.)

5: *Yamato.* Obviously, even in *TNG*, there sometimes isn't enough time to build new models: hence this so-called sister ship to the *Enterprise*. This vessel was already up to its E designation when encountered by its identical twin, and was destroyed by its taking a dump or something; either it's been in as many scrapes as its *manga* namesake, or it's just plain unlucky and ought to be decommissioned forthwith. Although if there was a Yamato F they could perhaps get a belated toy out of it.

6: *Stargazer.* The ship on which Picard attained his first command shares its name with a team of convention organisers. Picard's old ship is now out of commission – something else it shares with the team of convention organisers.

7: *Reliant.* Not as naff as it sounds – it hasn't got three wheels or anything.

8: *Excelsior.* This was rumoured to be replacing the *Enterprise* as the movie starship following the shocking destruction of every Trekker's most beloved space vessel in *The Search for Spock*. But, lo and behold, what should turn up at the end of *The Voyage Home* but a new *Enterprise*. Oh joy (and such a surprise too). (See also *EXCELSIOR*.)

9: *Pasteur.* Football-shaped medical ship (make that soccer ball-shaped if you're reading this in the US, and no doubt picturing a huge great rugby ball flying around outer space) commanded by Bev Crusher. Though, as it appeared in the now-impossible future of 'All Good Things', maybe it shouldn't count. And on the subject of those that probably don't count . . .

10: *Star Trek II* shuttle craft: Beautifully designed craft from the imagination of Matt Jeffries. It would almost have been worth putting up with a few adventures of Decker, Xon and the rest just to see this baby in action – but not quite. Any chance of a micro-machine anyway?

***

ARSE, CHAKOTAY'S: Presumably this bum flash was *Voyager*'s attempt to emulate the success of Picard's botty baring in *TNG*. In case you missed it, Chakotay's rear-end was, thankfully, sighted only briefly in the episode 'Tattoo'. As there was no evidence of any decoration on this part of his anatomy, we can only assume that the tattoo in question must be the one on his head: a design in honour of his father, Monolito off *The High Chaparral*.

ASCENSION CEREMONY: Masochistic Klingon ritual which involves being prodded with agony-inducing 'pain-stiks'. Well, as long as they're enjoying themselves. Oddly enough, Worf's son Alexander didn't fancy this Age of Ascension thing at all. Sensible lad.

'ASSIGNMENT: EARTH': *Original Series* episode guest-starring Robert Lansing (as Gary Seven), Terri Garr and a cat. 'Assignment: Earth' was intended to be the pilot for a potential spin-off series, though the option was not taken up. Just as well too: a *Star Trek* spin off? What a ridiculous idea.

***AURORA*:** Origami spaceship stolen by space hippies who no doubt appreciated the paper-folding skills involved in its construction.

AUTO-DESTRUCT: This facility is fitted aboard all Starfleet vessels, which is a bit of a mistake really. Starship captains can't resist the urge to initiate the sequence, ostensibly to thwart the attempts of some malevolent alien hell-bent on taking control of the ship. Thing is, we all know they're only doing it for dramatic effect and always intend to abort with only a few seconds remaining. However, this type of showing off could be risky and potentially fatal if, say, someone sneezes whilst giving the verbal command to halt the impending destruction. It perhaps also explains why we've never seen a starship captain with a stammer. Just look at Kirk, for example: he threatened to blow up the *Enterprise* several times before he finally cut things too fine in *Star Trek III*. Those nice-coloured lights and switches have often proved to be irresistible to Picard and Janeway too, as both have notched up an impressive list of near suicides – the latter even managed a dry run with a carbon-copy *Voyager* in 'Deadlock'. And as for Sisko, well, he'd been a captain for about five minutes before deciding to exercise the privilege that comes with the rank. He just couldn't wait to get on board the *Defiant* and set the auto-destruct sequence going.

B

BABYLON 5: Science fiction series which started at about the same time that the *Star Trek* franchise introduced a series set on a space station with a number in its title (*Deep Space Nine*, if you're having trouble working out which). Fans of *Bab 5* claim their show has better story-lining than *Star Trek*. Yeah, but they've only got one story-line and it takes them five years to get through it.

BADGES, STARFLEET INSIGNIA: Before they began to double as communicators (much to the disappointment of comedy writers, who lost the old communication devices as a source of hilarity – see list accompanying FRONT EAR, FINAL), the badges on Starfleet uniforms featured a variety of symbols denoting science, engineering and suchlike. We haven't a clue what Commodore Decker's uniquely distinctive badge was supposed to represent, though. Unlike Captain Tracey of the *Exeter*, he didn't seem the kind of guy who'd enjoy making new-age decorative jewellery, so perhaps it was a home-made birthday present from his little lad Will and the big softy didn't have the heart not to wear it. Similarly, Commodore Stocker – played by Charles Drake (no, not that one) – and his cronies at Starfleet wore flower-shaped brooches. We guess that this was sort of posh and sophisticated: the 23rd-century equivalent of sporting a carnation in the buttonhole.

BAJORAN RELIGION: Basis for several *Deep Space Nine* episodes, in which it has been established that the Bajorans have a tedious ritual for bloody well everything, from birth (an interminable succession of supposedly relaxing chimes) to death (the death chant is recited at funerals, but could equally well be named for the number of people in whom rigor mortis has no doubt set in whilst they sat through it). A more interesting Bajoran ritual was 'The Time of Cleansing' – or so we all thought, until it became apparent that it had nothing to do with Kira's bath night after all. Once *DS9* got going, storylines about the Bajorans' beliefs were dropped for the sensible reason that they were as dull as 'Masks'. They resurfaced in later seasons, by which time no one cared much any more.

BALDNESS: Although death is treatable in the 24th century (fortunately for Ensign Kim), to judge by the number of slapheads around, baldness isn't. Hard to believe really, so perhaps it's a fashion thing amongst captains, no doubt inspired by the ever-popular Jean-Luc Picard. Take Benjamin Sisko: perfectly sensible haircut whilst a commander, head as smooth as a baby's arse now he's a captain.* Blimey, they even program the trait into their holographic doctors now! And OK, so perhaps Janeway isn't bald yet but, let's face it, she certainly looks as if her entire head of hair could drop off if she ever moved too fast.

* *Yes, of course we were tempted to mention that other well-known captain and his alleged toupee, but we just didn't fancy a trip to court, OK?*

BALL, LUCILLE: Star of *I Love Lucy*, *Here's Lucy*, etc. We can't understand why she hasn't become a *Trek* icon: after all, without her Desilu company there might never have been a *Star Trek*. Wonder if she thought it was another comedy?

BANANA SPLIT: Because Wesley Crusher once expressed a liking for this dessert, *The Official Star Trek Fact Files* saw fit to print a recipe for it in their A–Z Database Access Point. Come on really, what kind of *Star Trek* A–Z worth its salt would ever include an entry for Banana Split?

BANDERA: *Voyager* crewman killed in a Kazon attack. We'd never seen him before, but he was Chakotay's best mate from way back, naturally. Citing the death of his friend,

Chakotay attempted to convince Janeway to change her approach to the scruffy aliens. His argument might have been a little more persuasive had he also mentioned that the same space battle had knocked at least four strands of her usually immaculate hairdo out of place.

BARBIE AND KEN: Although there's literally tons of *Star Trek* merchandise about, our favourite item ever must be the 30th anniversary gift set featuring America's most popular couple done up as characters from *TOS*.* The photographic illustration on the packaging is a bit misleading, though: while Ken makes a fairly passable Kirk in his mustard-coloured top,** Barbie, with her long blonde hair, red mini-dress, black tights and calf-length boots, doesn't really cut it as Mr Spock. Unless it's the off-duty version. Wouldn't it be great if Britain's most enduring TV icons were immortalised in a similar manner? Then, perhaps we could have the Ken Barlow Action Man and Sindy done up as Hilda Ogden.

It beats the Teenage Mutant Ninja Turtles' attempt to do the same thing, hands down.
**Although the lack of genitalia would tend to preclude most of Kirk's habitual activities, the hair is spot on.*

BARDAKIAN PRONGHORN MOOSE: Probably a moose from Bardakia with a pronghorn. But we neither know nor care.

BARE, PROFESSOR: Villain's dupe portrayed by Jadzia Dax in Bashir's James Bond-inspired holodeck fantasy. If ever we wanted a fictional character to live up to her name . . .

BASEBALL: Offshoot of the schoolgirls' game, rounders. Nowadays it is a sport in which the Americans excel; so much so that one of their teams always manages to win the World Series. In the future, it is Ben Sisko's favourite sport, although nobody else has played it for two hundred years – that bit at least is understandable.*

Though, in its defence, it is better than bloody cricket.

BASHIR, JULIAN, DOCTOR: Hmm, we can't really think of much to say about him, so we might as well use a bit from Wendy Rathbone's excellent, but unauthorized *Trek: A–Z**: 'Dark hair, dark eyes, and lean body add to his attraction. His British accent is icing on the cake.' Hey, you don't suppose she fancies him do you?

* *This is published in the UK by Voyager Books, which is a bit ironic because* Voyager *isn't in it.*

BATHROOM: Jonathan Frakes finally revealed, in the *Journey's End* documentary, that the *Enterprise* has only one, and it's at the very centre of the ship. This must make it pretty inconvenient to boldly go (cue canned laughter). Wouldn't you think, though, that there'd have to be different lavatories for all the separate races who might come on board? Apart from biological necessity, you'd surely want to avoid the embarrassment of standing at the urinals next to someone who sprays their excretions from their heads or something.

'BEAM ME UP, SCOTTY': By far the best *Star Trek* cliché not to have appeared in *Star Trek*. But hold on a minute, let's take a closer look at this oft-repeated anecdote. For a start, why would anyone make up a tedious stock catch-phrase for a series which, let's face it, has tons of them already (from 'a logical assumption, Captain' to 'I'm a doctor, not a [fill in the blank]' to the most common of all 'I want to direct')? And why are some fans so venomous in their rebuttals of the line's existence, considering that something very similar was said in almost every episode of *The Original Series*? It's as if, having suffered endless piss-takes in silence for decades, they've suddenly found one to which they can reply, 'Ah-ha-ha-ha, but you're completely wrong because Captain Kirk never said that, ever, so there! You know nothing, and *Star Trek* is still the best TV series ever made in the universe.' Perhaps. It does seem a bit pedantic, though, when you consider that 'Beam us up, Scotty' was indeed a regular cliché in *The Animated Series*. Protestations of 'But that doesn't count because Gene Roddenberry said so!' are likely to fall on deaf ears.

BEARD, RIKER'S: Conclusive proof that *Star Trek: The Next Generation* was popular enough to boldly go without the aid of a blatant Kirk clone. But it's odd that, when Data acquired an identical set of whiskers, they only provoked laughter. The other thing that's odd is how much thinner Riker looked when clean-shaven.

BELE AND LOKAI: Bitter enemies. The former, with the left side of his face white and the right side black, believed himself superior to the latter, whose visage bore the opposite colouration. Their mutual hatred highlighted the mindless absurdity of racial intolerance. Though we'd have been more sympathetic if they didn't both have ginger hair.

'BEST OF BOTH WORLDS, THE': Good as this two-part Borg adventure is, we tend towards the opinion that one video release was probably adequate, even if it was spread across two tapes. But then there was the special 'movie' version; like you can't really appreciate the episodes until you've seen them without credits in between. And then, of course, there was a special boxed set featuring classic Borg stories, which came in a cardboard replica of one of the sinister cyborgs' ships. Quite handy, then, that the said ships are, erm, box-shaped – certainly more so than a Federation tricorder, an over-sized replica of which was called upon to house 'City on the Edge of Forever' and 'The Trouble with Tribbles'. Very silly – and the latter episode could have been utilised so much better. We're still waiting for our special release of choice: a Tribble set, the cute, fuzzy exterior of which would peel back to reveal videos of all the classic monsters' appearances. The tribble is, they'd be bound to forget the crucial 'More Tribbles, More Troubles', wouldn't they?

BIBLE, THE: Bestselling novel about a carpenter's son, which – according to the American press – was spared the indignity of being reissued in Klingonese when its would-be translators encountered 'theological differences' on a summer camp. All together now: you sad bastards, you sad bastards, you sad bastards . . .

BOLTON WANDERERS: Our attempts to watch the *Voyager* episode 'Resistance' proved futile when, in the North-West, BBC2 replaced it with a documentary about this football club's departure from its ground of 102 years. For all we know, 'Resistance' could have been the all-time classic delta quadrant-based adventure, but now we'll probably never find out (buy the video? Get real!). To add insult to injury, BBC2 followed this with a preview of a programme on hot air ballooning which began with the words 'Space, the final frontier'. And then, just to rub salt into the wound, they put on their transporter pad '2' logo!

BOLTON WANDERERS (addendum): Bolton won the First Division championship and gained promotion to the Premier League, completing a clean sweep for North-West clubs in the 1996/97 season of English football, with Manchester United, Bury, Wigan and Macclesfield all winning their respective divisions. As for 'Resistance', well it was rescheduled in the region a few weeks later and the BBC bloody well took *The Saint* off for it! It turned out not to be the all-time classic *Voyager* episode (well, probably not . . . it's hard to tell which are the good ones). In it, Janeway supposedly gets dressed up as a tart, though she doesn't look much different from usual. She also meets some daft old bloke who thinks she's his little girl. Phew, what a loony.

BOND, JAMES BOND: One of many literary characters to which *Star Trek* has paid homage in its holodeck-set episodes: specifically *DS9*'s 'Our Man Bashir'. In their favour, this was less blatant than their predecessor *TNG*'s treatment of Conan Doyle's characters (see MORIARTY), which must have come as a great relief to Paramount's lawyers. Speaking of whom, they're a bit of a cheeky bunch of blighters really – they hate it when the reverse happens. (See CAPTAIN SMIRK.)

BORG QUEEN: An individual amongst the Borg, grafted onto the mythos when it was decided that a race with a collective consciousness was not clichéd enough to star in a Hollywood movie. What we needed was a strong humanoid villain, and if she could provide some sexual tension too, then so much the better.

BOTANY BAY: Discovered by the *Enterprise* crew in 'Space Speed', this 'sleeper ship' hailed from ... erm, the 1990s. Ahem. It contained the dormant body of Khan Noonian Singh who, it transpired, was the absolute ruler of over a quarter of the world from 1992 to 1996. Oh dear. He left Earth after losing the Eugenics Wars, in which whole populations were wiped out. Oops. What we want to know is, why wasn't any of this mentioned when the *Voyager* crew visited the 1990s in 'Future's End'?

BOTTLE SHOWS: Behind-the-scenes term for those episodes which, normally due to a lack of money, take place entirely on the ship/space station. An odd expression really, as you'd think it would be more a case of 'lost bottle'.

BRAIN REPLACEMENT OPERATION: Hilarious climax to the infamous self-parody that was 'Spock's Brain'. Spock's brain has been nicked by these aliens, right, and McCoy undergoes some sort of knowledge implant thingy to learn how to put it back. They stick the Vulcan's head through a hole in this partition so we can only see him from the forehead down and can well imagine that his scalp is gaping open. Then McCoy fumbles about in there and talks a load of old nonsense about reconnecting nerves, before his new-found knowledge disappears and he's forced to – wait for it – wake up Spock and ask him for help. Unperturbed by what's happening up top, and unable to see a thing anyway, Spock calmly talks McCoy through the closing stages of the process. And then he stands up, revealing no trace of scarring and a perfect head of hair. They just don't make them like that any more.

BUDGETS: Does *Deep Space Nine* have a bigger one than *Next Gen* had, or what? The reason we ask is: in the episode set in a future where Captain Sisko had vanished, a whole set of brand-new Starfleet uniforms were created for just one

21

brief scene on the *Defiant*. Yet in 'Yesterday's Enterprise', the crew of the *Enterprise C* had to make do with left-over movie costumes without the jerseys underneath. And we shan't even mention those pyjama suits in *The Motion Picture*.

BUTTONS, BELLY: Gene Roddenberry's egalitarian vision of the 23rd century saw women filling such responsible positions as communications officer and even second-in-command to Starfleet captains – just so long as they performed their duties in tight micro-minis or shiny bikinis. The latter mode of dress did, however, help to overcome one long-established American television taboo: that of navel baring – a particularly fine example being Nichelle Nichols' exposed midriff in 'Mirror, Mirror' (though you expect that kind of thing in a parallel universe story). By the 24th century, some women in *Star Trek* were becoming captains and even admirals – but the fashions of the day still allowed for the odd bit of tummy button flashing – most notably Denise Crosby in 'The Naked Now' (pity she didn't take the title more literally*) and Rosalyn Landor in 'Up the Long Ladder'.

* *Though, fortunately, we have that* Playboy *spread to allay the disappointment.*

C

'CAGE, THE': Rejected first pilot for *The Original Series*, which was later chopped up to form the basis of the two-part, Hugo Award-winning 'The Menagerie'. When the original version was reconstructed, fans were more than willing to purchase this unique piece of television history on video, even if certain scenes were only in black and white. They were marginally less willing to buy it again when the 'missing' colour footage turned out to exist after all (let's face it, there have been many less sound excuses for re-releasing *Star Trek* episodes on tape). But if only they'd waited, they could have just taped it when BBC2 featured it on their *Star Trek* night – then gone straight over it with *Men Behaving Badly*, or something else not too boring to watch on more than one occasion.

CAPTAIN'S CHAIR: Vital component of the *Enterprise* bridge, a newly constructed version of which was stolen from the set of *Generations* four days before filming began. Clearly this was the work of some sad anorak who wanted to be able to sit on the thing in his bedroom, dressed in Starfleet uniform and uttering profundities such as 'make it so' and 'warp factor eight, Mr Sulu'. If he'd thought more clearly, he'd have realised it's not even much of a collector's piece – at least, not half as much as it would have been if he'd waited for it to actually appear in *Star Trek* and to be graced by Patrick Stewart's buttocks. Perhaps he just wanted the perverse pleasure of seeing Picard standing throughout the movie and being able to say, 'That's down to me.' If so, he was disappointed: a replacement was built, with designers working around the clock to make it ready in time (though why they didn't just pop down to MFI is beyond us).

CAPTAIN SMIRK: Character from the *Star Wreck* series of unofficial parody novels. If, just by reading this name, you're sent into a fit of convulsive hysterical laughter, then these are the books for you because that's about as good as it gets. Imagine that: making jokes at *Star Trek*'s expense in order to sell books. Disgraceful! A completely dissimilar Kirk parody called, coincidentally, Captain Smirk also appeared on stage in the *Star Twek* series of plays in Salt Lake City. Paramount were more than a bit pissed off about this and issued a writ, claiming that the heroic status of its characters was being devalued, therefore causing financial loss. Yeah, sure.

CARDIGAN, JAKE: William Shatner's own science fiction creation in the *Tek* series. We can certainly appreciate Shatner's reluctance to lumber his character with a blatantly macho name, but Cardigan? There is apparently no truth in the rumour that Jake is to acquire a new partner, Bob Slippers.

CAR STICKERS: If your idea of being witty and urbane is to display the same piss-poor joke in the back of your car for several years, then these are for you. We've always thought car stickers should say things like: PEOPLE WHO HAVE THESE . . . DO IT WITH THEIR RIGHT HANDS, or MY OTHER CAR STICKER IS FUNNY. So, not surprisingly, there's a full range of *Star Trek* stickers available. Think carefully before you buy, though: once it's *in situ*, there'll be no concealing your proclivities from anyone. On the other hand, few people will risk stealing a motor that threatens to have a phaser on the dashboard, a festering Starfleet uniform rolled up in the boot and 'William Shatner – Live!' on the cassette player. But when you sell the car, how do you get the sticker back for your collection?

TEN HILARIOUS CAR STICKERS

1: I GROK SPOCK. Dunno what this means, but it sounds disgusting.

2: THIS VEHICLE TRAVELS AT WARPSPEED. Chortle!

3: KIRK/SPOCK IN '92. Dunno what this means either, unless it's a request for Kirk to give Spock a good grokking.

4: KIRK/SPOCK IN '96. So the first one must have sold well. Dare we suggest that KIRK/SPOCK IN '69 would have been a more welcome idea to some fans?

5: I AM FULLY FUNCTIONAL. A cheeky *double entendre* from that randy sex machine, Data.

6: DR McCOY DOESN'T MAKE HOUSE CALLS. These just get funnier.

7: MY OTHER VEHICLE IS A ROMULAN WARBIRD – and variations on the theme. Oh, our sides!

8: DON'T TAIL-GATE, THIS IS A FERENGI WAR CRUISER. A transparent deception.

9: WE WANT STAR TREK III. Obviously released before *Star Trek III*, 'cos who'd want it now?

10: I AM A TREKKIE. A definite no-no.

CATS: Animals surprisingly common in the *Star Trek* universe, though they can generally talk or transform into women and suchlike which, admittedly, isn't quite so common in the domestic variety. Even Data's otherwise unremarkable moggy, Spot, managed to change sex. On the other hand, Cat People – such as M'Ress from the planet Cait – are distressingly rare.

CENSORSHIP: Puritanical practice often applied by the BBC to *Star Trek* episodes. Their current reasoning is that some scenes aren't suitable to be shown at six o'clock. So why give it a six o'clock time-slot? *The Next Generation* came off particularly badly, with a whole episode – 'The

High Ground' – banned because of one line predicting a victory by the terrorist IRA. Better, we think, to have shown the thing and just laughed at it when it proved false (Steve wrote this bit, so shoot him – CH). Two seasons earlier, 'Conspiracy' was cut for no better reason than that it featured an exploding head (which we all saw anyway, in 'Shades of Gray'), and we were cheated of the long-awaited spear through Wesley's chest in 'Hide and Q' (though not in the repeat). But it goes back much further than that. Three episodes of *The Original Series* were skipped during the first ten thousand or so UK transmissions: 'The Empath' because of a tiny little bit of sadistic torture, 'Whom Gods Destroy' for its allegedly less-than-delicate treatment of loonies and 'Plato's Stepchildren' for some equally good reason, we're sure. 'Miri' was also banned after its first transmission when people complained about its scenes of child violence (nowadays, they'd have to cut news bulletins to keep that off the screen). At the time, though, rumour had it that one or more of these episodes had been kept off air because they failed to reach the BBC's quality threshold. Yeah, this from the corporation that made *Eldorado*? Right. And the catalogue of disgrace continues: they also restructured all episodes of *TOS* to remove the pre-titles sequences, in what can only have been a perverse attempt to annoy purists. And, for similar reasons, they showed several first-season *Next Gen* episodes in the wrong order, though rumour has it that someone had a quiet word in time to prevent Tasha Yar from making an unseemly return from the dead (well, before she was supposed to, anyway). Someone at the Beeb must be desperately trying to justify a pointless job, else why don't they just show the things as they were intended? Sorry, did that all seem a bit sad? Let's move on.

CHARLIE X: A descendant of Malcolm perhaps?

CHAT-UP TECHNIQUES: When Wesley developed a crush on Salia, he turned to some of his shipmates for advice on how to get off with her. Worf revealed that, in his culture, the Klingon females do a lot of roaring, clawing and throwing things at you, and the men read love poetry while ducking a lot. Riker and Guinan weren't much help either: they came out with some load of old nonsense about *Stars in their Eyes* or something. We'd have suggested he got right to the point and said something like 'A'right darlin' fancy a shag?' It wouldn't have worked, obviously, but that wouldn't have mattered since he strangely lost interest when she transformed into a huge-great- alien-Yeti-type-thing. Yeah, like he can afford to be picky.

'CHRISTMAS IS COMING – AND SO IS PATRICK STEWART': Distasteful blurb from the front cover of *DWB*'s Christmas '93 issue. Perhaps they didn't notice. Everyone else did. As it happened, the interview within was fairly tame: a disappointment to the hordes of female admirers whose hormones had been stimulated beyond endurance by a glimpse of the actor's bare buttocks in 'Chain of Command'.

CHRONOTON PARTICLES: Starfleet crews consistently look baffled when sensors detect these little buggers in the vicinity. By now, though, you'd think they'd just accept them as a sure sign that they've accidentally travelled in time again or that the past has been altered but for some freakish reason they've been unaffected and can remember the original history, which they'll now have to go back and restore. Best of all, they could wind up in the future where, chances are, one of them will discover that s/he is about to die horribly and will therefore have the chance to do something about it beforehand. Time travel is increasingly a feature of *Star Trek* plots: if it's not the *Next Gen* crew getting caught up in paradoxes, it's Sisko taking the place, almost *Quantum Leap*-style, of various doomed historical figures. And are all these stories logical and consistent in their application of physical laws? No, are they balls! Try wrapping your brain around this lot . . . oh, and see MOREAU, MARLENA for something a bit similar.

TEN TEMPORAL TWISTERS

1: In 'City on the Edge of Forever', McCoy supposedly changes history by saving Edith Keeler from a fatal car accident – and yet she only has the accident because of him in the first place, so he shouldn't have changed a thing. Should he?

2: 'Tomorrow is Yesterday' introduced the slingshot effect: the fantastic idea that you can travel into the past whenever you like by flying around a sun quite fast. They try to keep quiet about this one nowadays, going for such believable plot devices as the Bajoran Orb of Time instead. Ho-hum.

3: It's back to the Guardian of Forever and into Spock's past, when the Vulcan is wiped out of the time-lines (but, as always, sticks around with an unimpaired memory) in 'Yesteryear'. After a quick lecture from Kirk on how imperative it is not to tinker with the past, it suddenly occurs to Spock that his life was once saved by a 'cousin' who looked an awful lot like he does now. Best go and do that right away, then. Instant time loop!

4: Trekkers have wept blood trying to work out the chronology of Tasha Yar, so we won't bother. Suffice it to say that all relevant laws of temporal dynamics are superseded by the one, insurmountable *Star Trek* rule which states that no regular character shall stay dead. Oh, and for a full explanation of Sela Yar and all that, check out the *Fact Files* – though we can't help but feel that they didn't really need to use the same photo of Denise Crosby eight times to illustrate their theory.

5: Uh-oh. We've slingshot back to the 20th century for *The Voyage Home* and Scotty gives the formula for transparent aluminium to the man who, according to the history books, invented it. Do we know what that creates, people?

6: For a moment there, in *Generations*, we thought Picard had actually (gasp) made a mistake and let a world be destroyed. But no, just a quick trip to the past and he can put everything right. Trouble is, where's the first Picard when his future self (and that fat old bloke) pops up? Nowhere to be seen, that's where.

7: They probably don't want us to notice this, but Miles O'Brien is dead and his place has been taken by a counterpart from an alternative future – and a counterpart, at that, who shouldn't exist because his past self is now dead. Confused? Watch *DS9*'s 'Visionary' and you will be. Luckily, Bashir was on hand to deliver a quick pep talk, so O'Brien could quickly get back to normal without the very disturbing implications of his little adventure bothering him much.

8: 'Little Green Men' sees *Deep Space Nine*'s three major Ferengi characters crashing in a certain part of New Mexico in 1947. Trouble is, they look nothing like the so-called 'greys', which renders this Roswell story a mite less convincing than . . . well, than the Roswell stories done by nearly every other American science fiction series. We'll let it off though, 'cos it's quite fun.

9: For some reason, they seem to like using time travel in the movies and, in *First Contact*, we're into the old history-has-been-changed-but-a-bubble-of-chronotons-has-kept-the-*Enterprise*-as-it-was plot first used in 'City on the Edge of Forever'. This happens so much that we can't help but think history must have been re-written lots of times without our knowledge, as such an unlikely and convenient side-effect can't possibly have occurred on every occasion. We're all living in the wrong time-line. (See also COCHRANE, ZEFRAM.)

10: And here we go again, as the *Voyager* two-parter 'Future's End' has 29th-century technology falling into 20th-century hands and instigating the microchip revolution which allows 29th-century technology to exist. Aaargh! Also, a bloke from the future comes back to the present and changes his own past, which should result in another time loop. And as if that wasn't bad enough, they rip off the plot to 'Tomorrow is Yesterday' wholesale.

CIC VIDEOS: Some British fans got pretty upset and wrote incensed letters to magazines and things when CIC decided to put very-slightly-speeded-up episodes on their *Star Trek* tapes (starting with *Next Gen* season three). Others found the minute change in tempo a worthwhile trade for the better quality picture that the new conversion process allowed. And then there were those of us who just couldn't tell the difference and didn't give a toss.

CLASSIC: Word often used to distinguish the first incarnation of *Star Trek* from *The Next Generation* etc. In this context, however, 'classic' is used as a description of something long established and not, as per its more commonly used definition, of something with class. Our preferred nomenclature is *Star Trek: The Original Series*, particularly as this abbreviates to *TOS* – although we might well call it *Star Trek* or *Original Star Trek* at various junctures (we just don't care) – this way we can avoid such ridiculous phrases as 'In the classic episode "Spock's Brain" . . .'

CLIFFHANGERS: Innovative way to end seasons of *Star Trek* – or at least it would have been if *Blake's 7* hadn't done it already. Although it was usually the case in that series that those climactic episodes were intended to end the programme for good; trouble is, it kept coming back. Lucky the regular cast were all wiped out at the end of series four (series D if you're sad) or we'd never have seen the back of it. The lengthy wait notwithstanding, two-parters work well in the *Star Trek* format. Let's face it, even Captain Picard would struggle to smash a conspiracy that went right to the heart of Starfleet, in only 45 minutes (or, at best, an hour with advert breaks). Also, you can rely on these season-linking adventures to be pretty spectacular. Though, as with all *Star Trek*, the scripts vary in quality, so you end up with all-time classics like 'Best of Both Worlds' part one and disappointing efforts like 'Best of Both Worlds' part two. Now, we hear (it hasn't been on yet) that *Voyager* is to pull out all the stops with something called 'Scorpion'. Apparently, bigness is to be the order of the day: big effects, big aliens, big guest stars (that fat bloke off *Sliders*), and at least fifteen Borg Cubes. Blimey, they'll have to buy a family-size box of Oxos to do that.

'CLUES': The ship's crew awake to find that it's somewhat later than they expected: they have lost some time, and at least one of them has a broken limb. Against the advice of their mechanical colleague, they set about recovering their memories of the stolen moments, only to find that they were better off not knowing. Oops, sorry, forgot what series we were covering for a moment there: we were giving you a synopsis of *Red Dwarf*'s 1988 adventure 'Thanks for the Memory', and not the entirely dissimilar 1991 *Next Generation* episode to which some fans have inexplicably compared it. We'd hate to repeat the utterly libellous speculation which surrounded the two programmes, except to recall that we were once present when a desperate Trekker asked Hattie Hayridge (*Red Dwarf*'s Holly – well, one of them) if the entire cast of that series had flown to America to watch *Star Trek* and steal its story-lines. Yeah, and they went back in time too! Comparisons between *Red Dwarf*'s 'Better Than Life' and *Next Gen*'s 'The Game' only added fuel to the fire – but still, the claims of *Red Dwarf* co-creator Rob Grant that *Star Trek* only did time paradox stories after they did seems to be taking it a bit far.

COCHRANE: *Voyager* shuttle craft that became the first ever vessel to cross the Warp Ten threshold. An appropriate name really, wasn't it (see COCHRANE, ZEFRAM if you don't know why)? Could it be that, by a huge coincidence, *Voyager* actually had a craft by that name or did they just change an existing one from *El Baz* or *Galileo* or whatever? The craft seemed strangely unaffected by going so fast – unlike its pilot, Tom Paris, who had quite a bad time of it: first he died, then he came back to life with two hearts (a bit like Doctor Who) and an alopecia problem (a bit like . . . erm, no, we'd better not say). Finally he turned into an amphibious fish-thing and had to have sex with his captain. Not one of his better days. Still, it's no excuse for leaving his three newborns to fend for themselves on that jungle planet. Why, he oughta be reported to the Child Support Agency. And some mother Kate Janeway turned out to be.

TEN MINOR CONTINUITY LINKS BETWEEN THE VARIOUS TREK STRANDS, MUCH LOVED BY SAD FANS

1: Willard Decker was the son of Commodore Matthew Decker and a chip off the old block too, judging by his ability to fall out with Kirk and then wind up dead.

2: The Mirror Universe Kirk advanced to captaincy by assassinating Christopher Pike. If only they'd mentioned somewhere that Pike did likewise by bumping off Robert April, it would have been the icing on the cake.

3: A boxing poster seen in *DS9*'s 'Past Tense' part two, identical to one seen in 'City on the Edge of Forever', just makes that episode.

4: John Colicos, the original *Star Trek* Klingon, must have been a bit perturbed when asked to don a lumpy forehead to reprise the role of Kor (twice) for *Deep Space Nine*.

5: In the time-stream in which Harry Kim became a starship design specialist, he was awarded a, wait for it, Cochrane medal of excellence for outstanding advances in warp theory.

6: Captain Sulu sponsored Chakotay for entry into Starfleet Academy. And he still got in!

7: Kirk and McCoy's defence lawyer in 'The Undiscovered Country' was an ancestor of Worf's and was also played by Michael Dorn. That's quite a good one, that is.

8: This one isn't so good. Riker's dad survived an attack by the same web-spinning Tholians as seen in *TOS*. Even the most ardent Trekkies would be hardpressed to get excited about that. To improve it a bit, we could point out that the Tholians got a couple of other mentions in *TNG*, then top it off by referring to the Tholian silk that Sisko got for Kassidy . . . Nope,

34

still boring. How about Automatic Unit 3947 telling Torres he'd like to be acquainted with Data. Any better?

9: Spock's childhood sehlat mentioned in 'Journey to Babel' actually turns up in the animated classic 'Yesteryear' and is called I'Chaya. In fact, come to think of it, the entire fantastic run of *The Animated Series* is chock-full of well-considered and respectful references to its live-action forerunner. Dunno why they bothered, though.

10: 'Trials and Tribble-ations' featured a very brief cameo from David Gerrold, writer of 'The Trouble with Tribbles', whose intended walk-on part in the original episode never happened.

COCHRANE, ZEFRAM: Architect of warp-propulsion technology, though not without some help from the *Enterprise* crew, which must take the shine off his achievement. He envisaged a future with piles of cash and similar quantities of naked girls; he wound up with a love-sick alien and a sensible haircut. To his credit, the stress didn't seem to age him – quite the opposite, in fact. Cochrane originally appeared in 'Metamorphosis', but came back 30 years later in *First Contact*. As so much time had elapsed, the producers were obviously hoping that people would have forgotten he was supposed to hail from Alpha Centauri, not Earth. They hadn't.

COLLINS, NGHAIRE: Trekker and one-time star of BBC2's *Video Nation Shorts*. Disregarding an unwritten law and risking derision from her peers, she took a bold step: rather than purchase an over-priced official import, she sewed together her own Captain Kirk top to wear at conventions. The end result was easily on a par with the so-called authentic merchandise, so a victory for common sense we think (well, as far as going round dressed as someone from *The Original Series* can be considered sensible, that is).

CONVENTIONS: Gatherings of like-minded fans. They exist in some form or other for most things that can be described as 'cult', but especially for science fiction TV shows. However, *Star Trek* events are quite different from their *Doctor Who* and *Red Dwarf* counterparts. For a start, the usual convention pastime of sniggering at the small group of tragic attendees who have come dressed as characters from the series is cruelly reversed, so that anyone out of Starfleet uniform might as well be stark naked. And if you're expecting a plethora of guest speakers, you're likely to be disappointed. Most of the series' actors live in America (of course) and charge such exorbitant appearance fees that you feel you should be using the money to buy a small house instead. Bizarrely, some organisers get around this by inviting people who have nothing to do with the programme at all. Gareth Thomas is a current favourite, on the grounds that he once said he'd like to be in a *Star Trek* episode and that he did star in *Blake's 7* which is a bit like it really. But, for the most part, *Star Trek* events consist of three expensive days on which not a lot happens (although you can spend even more cash on the insane amount of stuff in the obligatory merchandise room). The recent exceptions were those events organised by a company called Stargazer, who pumped a sinful amount of dosh into getting decent turn-outs from the stars for once. Sadly, they were otherwise crap. Stargazer tragically went bust after cancelling an event at Wembley Arena – at which the cast of *First Contact* were due to appear – at the last minute. They even told one or two of their potential attendees.

CRITICAL: The usual state of the containment fields. (See also HULL and BREACH.)

CROSSOVERS: Not much to say about these really. You'd expect the various *Star Trek* strands to intersect more often, but it seems they can't afford to pay two whole casts to appear in one episode. That's why the entire crew of the *Enterprise* or the *Voyager* can wander around *Deep Space Nine* for hours and see just one member of staff, and why only Picard turned out to see Miles O'Brien off when he was transferred. Not to mention that the *Enterprise D* crew have to encounter their illustrious predecessors one at a time, as and when they can be afforded. Books and comics, of course, are exempt from actors' fees and can produce as many crossovers as they like. But who cares?

CURZON: Dax's previous host. Thanks to an unusual Trill capability, his memories were removed from the symbiont and telepathically placed in Odo. They were both happy with the arrangement as it allowed Curzon to go out on the razz, while Odo got a proper nose out of the deal. Most of the other *DS9* regulars offered to temporarily play host to earlier, er, hosts too. We know they're all good mates and everything, but would you lend Jadzia your body for a couple of hours? . . . We can't believe we've just asked that question.

CUSTOMARY JOKE AT THE END OF THE EPISODE: Granted: it's tough in space and you can expect a certain number of casualties. But no matter how many crew members in red shirts have bitten the dust in the previous 50 minutes, Kirk, Spock and McCoy always manage to overcome their grief enough to crack a joke or two. Even the ostensibly more enlightened Picard and co. do it. Callous bastards.

'*DAD'S ARMY* IN SPACE': Since it was on Channel 5, chances are you missed this comment from Jack Docherty, describing the later film outings of the original crew. If Jack finds guests as hard to come by as an audience, he'd better stop insulting people he might one day need to fill a slot.

'DANNY CAN'T CLING ON TO HIS KLINGONS': Terribly witty headline in the *Daily Star* which must have gone a long way towards cheering up the focus of the story, Danny Nelson, who'd just had his entire £17,000 *Star Trek* collection stolen. 'Crooks beamed up to his flat . . . and left only space in place of spacemen,' quipped the paper. Danny, who watched two 'Trekkie movies' every night before they were nicked, said, 'I live, breathe and sleep *Star Trek* – but it's made it difficult to get girlfriends. They think "My God, we've got a freak here." ' Women, eh?

DARTS: Game enjoyed by Bashir and O'Brien that seems to have changed hardly at all since the present day – apart, that is, for those noisy flashing lights around the board's edge. It's easy to imagine becoming very irritated by that and wanting to throw things at the dartboard. A very sensible addition, then.

DATA: Dunno why they make all that fuss about him. Captain Kirk copped off with more sophisticated androids years before. Still, he may just be a soulless automaton but he's still got more of a discernible personality than the rest of his shipmates. You can bet Tasha Yar wasn't attracted to his devilish good looks when she used him, literally, as a sex machine.

'DATA WAS AVAILABLE, I TOOK HIM, WE CAME':
Line spoken by Shelby in 'The Best of Both Worlds'. It has become a source of amusement for fandom as, taken in the wrong context, it sounds a bit rude. Well actually, it sounds a bit rude in almost any context.

DAVIDSON, JIM: Cheeky Cockney-style comedian and latest host of *The Generation Game*. *The Next Generation Game*, more like. Jim is a shameless Trekker: he thinks nothing of coming on the show dressed in his *ST:TNG* pyjamas. References abound and sometimes, as he hands over their *Generation Game* jackets, he'll wave off the dejected losers with a chirpy 'Live long and prosper'. Consolation indeed.

DEATH SEAT: Euphemistic term given to the front-starboard chair on the *Enterprise* (behind the scenes, of course). Red shirt or no, if someone gets posted here they aren't long for this world – or any other. Presumably that's why it's often empty, as volunteers must be few and far between. The most recent casualty was Lt. Hawk, whose death in *First Contact* was revealed by actor Neal McDonough in interviews long before the event, on the grounds that we'd all guessed anyway. It shows Picard up as a right bastard, though, that he should take the newest member of his bridge crew out gallivanting on the side of the ship, knowing full well the mortality rate for such people. He even murdered the hapless Hawk himself when the Borg failed to do the job. When Picard made his decision that death is better than assimilation into the Borg collective, he must have been forgetting his own complete return to good health after just such an experience.

TEN HANDY HINTS FOR *STAR TREK* CHARACTERS

1: Aspiring officers: politely decline to be transferred to the *Enterprise*, as subsequent promotion to officer rank will mean death (unless you are a precocious teenage technical whizz). If you feel you can't pass up the opportunity, you must at least insist upon choosing your own shirt colour.

2: *Deep Space Nine* personnel: if something weird and baffling happens on the station – particularly if it concerns your own past – look around immediately for a nearby alien visitor who will be gurning enigmatically towards camera to the accompaniment of a drawn-out musical sting. Pursue him for any explanations required.

3: Original *Enterprise* crew: if Captain Kirk starts to act out of character – by giving up his macho posturing and pursuit of women, for example – assume he's been replaced by yet another evil *doppelgänger* and shoot the bugger post-haste.

4: Ladies: if a handsome, charming Starfleet commander called Riker starts coming on to you, run for it. A dalliance with him will invariably lead to death, possession or brainwashing by the end of the episode. Be warned.

5: All 24th-century Starfleet members: try to get into the habit of saying 'Computer, end program' at least once a day, in case you have been trapped unawares in a pernicious holodeck scenario.

6: Would-be lotharios: if hoping to cop off with a crewmate, skip all that courting, foreplay, etc. and just get straight down to it. This is essential as, by the end of the episode, some sort of amnesia-inducing fluke – like a trip through parallel dimensions or an unexpected transmogrification into another species – will have restored the status quo and you'll have to start all over again.

7: Starship commanders/captains: promotions should only be accepted if they don't carry a consequent transfer to a starship without its own show. Who wants to be an admiral anyway, if it means you can't be on telly each week?

8: Scientists: don't waste years of research and toil on trying to find a cure for blindness, when a simple slidey thing from a girl's hair – wrapped about the face – will alleviate the symptoms just as well.

9: Medical staff: if someone claims to have discovered a new life form, try not to laugh in their face as you'll only look stupid later. This applies no matter how ridiculous the assertion: you might wish to harp on about what defines life for an hour or so, but the bottom line is that everything from androids to nanites to emergency medical programs to starships seems to qualify.

10: Students of Klingonese: get a life!

DEBRIS: When the *Enterprise* discovered a piece of old spaceship with only the word NASA and the Stars and Stripes flag painted on it providing the tiniest of clues to its origins, Data's detailed analysis soon revealed that in fact it came from Earth. Wow, he's good.

DEMILITARIZED ZONE, THE: Popular combat site.

DENEBIANS: The inhabitants of Deneb V are a fair-minded bunch to be sure. When it comes to the unpleasantness of handing out punishments, they even offer their prisoners a choice: death by electrocution, death by gas, death by phaser, death by hanging . . . We have yet to discover which method the Federation prefer, although the death penalty most certainly does exist in their enlightened society – just listen to what the M-5 has to say in 'The Ultimate Computer'. In 'The Menagerie', Admiral Mendes admits it too, but claims that the ultimate sanction is only taken in the face of the most heinous crime imaginable: unauthorised contact with Talos IV.

DESALLE: He had three *TOS* outings, but we don't know much about him really. He must have been good though because he was given command of the *Enterprise* when all the senior officers beamed down to Pyris VII for a spot of trick or treating in the none-too-scary episode that was 'Catspaw'.

DINKY TOYS: UK toy manufacturers of the only piece of *Star Trek* merchandise to come close to the Barbie and Ken

44

Gift Set: a die-cast model of the original *Enterprise*. This 1976 toy fired photon torpedoes; admittedly, its little yellow plastic discs didn't have quite the destructive capabilities of the real thing, but aimed at someone's eye they could deliver a nasty sting. Even better, concealed within the hangar bay was a little shuttle craft (presumably the *Galileo 7*). And just when we all thought that was as good as it could possibly get, it was issued in a boxed set with a Klingon Battle Cruiser. Heaven.

DSN: A recently coined abbreviation for *Deep Space Nine*, being increasingly foisted upon us by pedants. We have opted to use the far more apposite and pleasing *DS9* instead.

DS9: Gene Roddenberry would never have approved of this slightly darker variation of *Star Trek*, in which the regulars have been known to display envy, anger, and greed, and worst of all, Chief O'Brien sometimes has the sleeves of his uniform rolled up!

$$\boxed{\text{E}}$$

EARHART, AMELIA: Real-life aviator whose plane mysteriously disappeared without trace over the South Seas in 1937. People assumed she'd crashed into the ocean, but in fact she was kidnapped by an alien race known as the Briani (not to be confused with the Indian curry), transported to the other side of the galaxy and put in stasis, only to be awoken, Buck Rogers-like, centuries later by the crew of *Voyager*. Phew, that's that mystery solved then.

EARTH ORBIT: Current location of Gene Roddenberry's ashes – some of them, anyway – which were sent into space as a tribute to the man who shared his dream of space travel with us all. And the fact that his family forked out five thousand dollars for the privilege may have had something to do with it too. Accompanying him was the late drug guru Timothy Leary, who apparently fancied one last far-out trip. While we can see the appeal of being out among the stars, this seems a drastic method by which to achieve the ambition, and probably not the best way to appreciate the experience either. Quite appropriately for the creator of *Star Trek*, Roddenberry will stay up there for just a few years before crash-landing. No doubt, a horde of fans will then petition him to do the same thing all over again.

EDEN: Fantastically beautiful planet, so we were told. And, admittedly, it wasn't too bad for a studio set with some plastic flowers and fruit trees on it. We think the planet's unusual atmospheric conditions must have been responsible for causing Kirk's insignia badge to jump back and forth from one side of his chest to the other. Unless you can come up with a better explanation. See also McCOY'S MAGIC BLUE SHIRT for a similar cock-up.

EDUCATION: What a wonderful thing this will become in the future. Mind completely wiped by an alien machine? Not to worry: a few lines of 'See the dog run', and you'll be back to your old self in no time. It's hard to imagine the realistic impact of such an experience on Uhura, particularly as it was hardly dwelled upon at the time (in 'The Changeling'). Even if you accept the re-education thing, she must have emerged with no memories of her former life and no emotional attachment to those details which could be related to her. It's a bit crappy really, isn't it? Still, so long as she remembered how to say 'Hailing frequencies open' and sing every so often, who'd notice?

ELEEN: There wasn't really anything that amusing about the *TOS* episode 'Friday's Child' – well, apart from the Capellan's costumes, which were even sillier than the token Klingon's golden tank-top. But what was unusual, nay almost unique, about this particular episode was that Captain Kirk failed to pull! Eleen was determined not to let him cop a feel; OK, she was heavily pregnant and her husband had just been killed, but really, what was wrong with the woman? McCoy fared a little better, after reassuring her that it was all right for a doctor to touch (what a great line). Luckily for us, this meant he could later utter the immortal phrase 'I'm a Doctor, not an escalator' as he assisted her to clamber up some rocks. Speaking of which, Kirk and co. only went to Capella IV to obtain a mining treaty, but ended up purposefully burying a bunch of its inhabitants under a rock-slide, then seeing off a few more of them with home-made arrows. Surely the Prime Directive doesn't allow that – especially the latter, as bow-and-arrow technology had yet to be discovered on that world.

EMMY: Prestigious US TV award deservedly won by *Star Trek: The Animated Series*. Did *The Original Series* ever get one? No. Did it deserve one? We don't think so.

'ENDLESS CLICHÉS AND SHALLOW CHARAC-TERS': A description of the novel *Hotel Royale*, a book which well-intentioned aliens used as the basis for what they believed was an accurate recreation of Earth. All right then, this explains the plot and people in *TNG*'s 'The Royale'. What excuse have all the other episodes got?

ENTERPRISE: Fans campaigned long and hard to get NASA to name their first spaceshuttle after the famous ship from TV's *Star Trek*. Their efforts paid off all right, and the administration duly obliged; trouble was, that particular shuttle was never intended to go into space at all, which rather defeated the object. *The Motion Picture* attempted to rectify this mistake by featuring a *Voyager 6* probe, no doubt imagining that NASA would have to launch one eventually. Instead, they spitefully curtailed the *Voyager* programme after only two missions. Perhaps they feared that fanatics might try to make *Star Trek* come true by sabotaging the real-life *Voyager 6*'s guidance systems. Anyway, Paramount eventually found the best solution. By simply christening their latest flagship *Voyager*, after something that had been in space already, they avoided lots of unnecessary aggravation. It seems unlikely that NASA will adopt the name *Deep Space Nine* for one of their future projects, but who knows? With another concerted letter-writing campaign, it could happen.

ENTERPRISE PHONE: The ideal purchase if you're one of those sad bastards determined to relate every aspect of their lives to *Star Trek* in some way. Now you can speak to your friends on an officially licensed product with William Shatner's autograph etched into it . . . oh sorry, forgot you don't have any friends. Never mind, you can use it to call your local SF store and order more sad junk. The phone is an authentic replica of the actual *Enterprise* – well, except that the real one doesn't have a bloody-great ear-piece under the saucer section or a big, black cable attached to its rear-end. Nor does it have to split into two pieces every time it receives a communication.

EUGENE: Tom Paris's middle name, and also, not so coincidentally, the full first name of *Star Trek* creator Gene Roddenberry. A case of gratuitous name-dropping really, not that Gene wasn't capable of doing that all by himself. His middle name was Wesley, you know – hence Commodore Wesley in 'The Ultimate Computer' and young Master Crusher in *The Next Generation*. We confidently predict that a future *Star Trek* series will detail the exploits of a Captain Rod N Berry.

EVEN-NUMBERED *STAR TREK* MOVIES: Those which, according to fans, are consistently better than the ones in between. You'd think Paramount would've realised this by now and adopted a new numbering system accordingly. Or perhaps they should just commission two scripts for each film and chuck the first one in the bin.

***EVERYTHING I NEEDED TO KNOW I LEARNED FROM WATCHING STAR TREK*:** A useful book to read, we reckoned, just in case we ever found ourselves aboard a 23rd-century starship – it could happen. But as soon as we reached the bit where the author reveals that, just like Captain Kirk, he never married, it became clear that this wasn't really the book for us after all. No offence, like.

***EXCELSIOR*:** Hikaru Sulu must have really cheesed off his senior crewmates: after they'd turned down every promotion going and Starfleet finally got around to offering one to the lowly Lieutenant, he broke all the rules by accepting the captaincy of the *Excelsior* and leap-frogging his mates up the career ladder. It certainly caused bad feeling in real life . . . well, allegedly. George Takei, allegedly, criticised William Shatner for, allegedly, trying to muck up his promotion scene as, allegedly, he was jealous of Sulu's progress (did we mention that these are just other people's allegations?). Shatner, in turn, claimed he'd only warned Takei against transferring off the *Enterprise* as it might entail a limited role in subsequent adventures. He was right, too: it soon became difficult for writers to involve Sulu in story-lines (just look what a cock-up they made of bringing back Worf in *First Contact*). But perhaps

Takei had his eye, even then, on the long-term possibility of an *Excelsior* series, for which he has been pushing. The *Voyager* episode 'Flashback' gave us an idea of just how entertaining such a series would be,* and there have also been some solo Sulu adventures released on audio cassette and CD, starring George Takei. Alas, the first of these was entitled 'Cacophony' and was thus easily overlooked by fans in the belief that it was a Leonard Nimoy record (see 'HIGHLY ILLOGICAL').

* *Come on, own up, who had a sneaky look at* The Undiscovered Country *to see if they could spot Tuvok in the* Excelsior *scenes? You'd have more chance of spotting Christian Slater in the* Voyager *episode.*

TEN CROSSOVER-TYPE ANNIVERSARY CELEBRATIONS THAT WOULD HAVE BEEN MORE ENTERTAINING THAN 'FLASHBACK'

1: 'More Trials, More Tribble-ations'. Mirroring *DS9*'s brilliant 30-year tribute, this would have seen the *Voyager* crew travelling back in time to land on the cartoon *Enterprise* of the mid-23rd century. Hilarity would have ensued when, spotting a human being, Neelix asked why he resembled an animation cell. Janeway would have gone red and dismissed it as an embarrassing chapter of our history.
2: Kirk could have been returned from the dead. It's going to happen, so it may as well have been in the anniversary year. And we'll just bet that William Shatner's got a few ideas for a script knocking about at home.
3: Hey, they could have brought back the lava-men from 'Savage Curtain', couldn't they, as a tribute to the unsung rocks of *The Original Series*? When has there ever been an alien monster more threatening? More dangerous? More amusing?
4: The 30th anniversary was surely a time for bridge-building between all the various *Star Trek* strands, and so guest appearances by M'Ress, Arex, etc. would hardly have gone amiss.

5: Or they could have brought back the giant Spock clone from 'The Infinite Vulcan'.

6: We could have had a proper *Voyager/ Original Series* crossover. How fascinating it would have been to watch Janeway and Kirk's first meeting. Would Kate remain an upright, respectable monogamist, true to her absent partner? Naw, Kirk'd get to poke her, wouldn't he?

7: 'The Five Doctors'. Taking a leaf from *Doctor Who*'s ten-yearly nostalgia-fest, this would have seen the holographic Doctor unable to cope with a virus and calling up holograms of Starfleet's finest medical personnel to offer advice. Crusher and Pulaski could have had that catfight we've all wanted for so long, and the latter would have found out just how similar she is to McCoy. Bashir would have done something interesting too, we shouldn't wonder.

8: Or, if the budget stretched to it, we could have had the more original 'The Six Doctors', giving us another chance to see the divine Christine Chapel. In fact, sod it, that virus should kill the entire crew and this could be the basis for a new series.

9: But the ultimate tribute would have been the formation of a new crew, using established but under-utilised favourites. The captain could have been someone well used to serving as Number One on a distinguished ship. She would have been assisted by an experienced doctor, a counsellor – perhaps Betazoid – a security officer with cat-like agility and senses, and of course a talking computer. We can think of just the characters, but no doubt you have your own ideas.

10: Simplest of all, Chekov and Uhura could have appeared in the 24th century as well as Sulu, just to complete the set. We might even have forgiven 'Flashback' if Uhura had been in it as planned.

EXHIBITION, THE UK TRAVELLING *STAR TREK*: An unparalleled collection of props and sets, which even gave you the opportunity to stand on the bridge of the *Enterprise* itself if it came to your town. It did actually reside for several months in Manchester and, had we only known that we'd be stuck with writing this book, we'd have gone and seen it too. Trouble is, they advertised for people to help run the thing and made it clear they only wanted the saddest of the sad. Local news bulletins showed scenes of ranks of Klingons and Starfleet officers queuing around the block for the purpose of procuring a job that would legitimise their antics. If ever a company psychiatrist was needed, this was the place.

EXTRA-STOUT SYNTH ALE: Bevy enjoyed by Miles O'Brien – space Guinness.

F

FANCY DRESS: Tired of going to conventions dressed as the same old Klingon? Well, why not try putting on a blonde wig, sticking a white woolly sock on your arm with button eyes sewn on it, and go as 'Lights of Zetar' co-author Shari Lewis and her once-popular glove puppet Lambchop.

FASCINATING: Mr Spock's considered opinion of practically everything he ever encountered.* Which was nice for him and must have made the time pass much faster on his five-year mission aboard the *Enterprise*. In fact, it probably seemed more like three.

* Though he might say 'incredible' if the universe was about to blow up or something.

'FATE PROTECTS FOOLS, LITTLE CHILDREN AND SHIPS NAMED *ENTERPRISE*': Line spoken by Riker in 'Contagion' and quoted in every *Star Trek* reference work going, so we thought we'd keep up the tradition.

FATE, TEMPTING: 'In the history of my people,' says Odo in 'The Adversary', 'no Changeling has harmed another. I'd hate to be the first.' Then, for good measure, he adds: 'I've never found it necessary to fire a weapon or take a life; I don't intend to start now!' Do you know what he does before the end of that very episode? Yeah, that's right. How did you guess?

FERENGI RULES OF ACQUISITION, THE: The Ferengi themselves would have been proud of this great money-making venture from Pocket Books. You might expect it to be a complete guide to the profiteering race's famous pearls of wisdom, but no – it simply restates all the rules we've already heard in *Deep Space Nine*. There are even spaces to fill in later ones yourself as the series progresses, which leads us to conclude that it would be far cheaper to just do this from the start – or to copy them out of one of the several factual books in which they're listed alongside additional snippets like complete episode guides, behind-the-scenes details, etc.

TEN GREAT WAYS TO CASH IN ON THE *STAR TREK* FRANCHISE

1: Watch a few episodes, write down what you see and market the results as an exclusive factual guide to the series.

2: Stick the original logo on a few bits of tat like calendars, bookmarks, mouse mats, pop-up greetings cards, etc. and sell at vastly inflated prices. Repeat, using the *TNG*, *DS9* and *Voyager* logos. See SQUARED PAPER for a few good suggestions.

3: Release a set of trading cards but make some far rarer than others. Watch the cash roll in as fans purchase hundreds of duplicates in the hope of one day finding a full set. Once sales begin to drop, bring out another set and so on, *ad infinitum*. As interest flags, try calling them 'game cards' and passing them off as something different.

4: Start up a publishing company and release a billion or so tie-in novels. Perhaps you could sound out some *Star Trek* stars to see if, in addition to their acting and directorial skills, they might also happen to be talented writers. You'll find that many of them are.

5: Marry the producer of *Star Trek*, then audition for multiple roles in each new off-shoot.

6: Find some way to become peripherally involved with the franchise for a while, then accept tons of convention

7: Release a genuinely desirable piece of merchandise – for the sake of argument, let's say a six-foot-long model of the *Enterprise* – which will have fans drooling insatiably and prepared to cash in their own grandmothers for the chance to own one. Then – and this is the clever bit – charge one and a half grand for it.

8: Self-publish a couple of cheap magazines: stick *Star Trek* photos on some covers and run the odd episode guide and padded-out interview that consists of a few words snatched with the subject in question when he was signing his book in Waterstone's.

9: Make yourself indispensable as an actor, then demand a five million dollar increase in your fee.

10: Obtain the rights to *Star Trek* and create several new programmes bearing its name. They don't need to resemble *The Original Series* in any way: if preferred, they can be just network-friendly formulaic stuff. Either way, you'll inherit an army of fans who'll ensure lucrative merchandising and syndication deals. They might slag you off a bit on the internet, but you'll be making a fortune out of them, so who cares?

FINGER, MIDDLE: The absence of such a digit is a notable feature of Jimmy Doohan's right hand, which must've made it hard to respond to Shatner's alleged jibes about him. Miraculously, the finger grew back for close-up shots in which Scotty operated consoles. He must have kept a spare one in the transporter room for emergencies.

FIRST ADVENTURE, THE: An early working-title for *Star Trek VI*, which would have featured the *TOS* crew as youngsters at Starfleet Academy. Paramount were still feeling stung by the fact that *Star Trek V* had been a bit crap and unpopular, and this would have allowed them to bring back their most famous characters and still have them look remotely capable of sustaining adventure of any sort (they'd have saved cash too). The adult Kirk, Spock, et al. would have appeared only in a brief framing sequence – so imagine Paramount's surprise when the actors concerned didn't think much of the idea. William Shatner, in particular, protested that he looked as young then as he did when he first appeared in *Star Trek*. Which, sadly, is one of those things that we don't dare pass comment on. In the end, then, it was girdles out and wigs on for a final proper outing of the original team. But a far more entertaining outcome went unconsidered: a full-length movie sequel to a later incarnation of *Star Trek* would have solved all the studio's problems at a stroke and allowed a dignified return of the ultimate science fiction heroes, unfettered by the restraints of passing years. Animation cells don't age!

FIRST INTER-RACIAL KISS ON US TELEVISION, THE: Afro-American Nichelle Nichols' on-screen kiss with William Shatner caused quite a stir when first broadcast on American television. Can't think why, what with Captain Kirk's relentless pursuit of anything vaguely female from just about any species you'd care to mention. Doubtless, the producers just thought his macho image would be threatened if he didn't get to snog the lovely Uhura. But doesn't it give out the wrong message that he had to be mind-controlled to do it?

FLAHERTY: First Officer aboard the USS *Aries*. He had the ability to speak forty languages including Romulan and Klingon, which sets something of a standard for real-life, sad Trekkies. Despite such talents, though, Starfleet passed him over for promotion in favour of a reticent Will Riker. Nor was he ever accorded the privilege of an on-screen appearance, which just goes to prove the old adage that Flaherty will get you nowhere.

FLINT: Not only did he claim to be immortal but he reckoned he'd been both Brahms and Leonardo da Vinci too. Oh yeah, Brahms and Liszt more like.

FLOGGING A DEAD HORSE: See *Voyager*.

FOCUS, SOFT: Flattering camera technique which not only disguises an actress's facial lines and blemishes but also gives her a kind of ethereal look. This was often employed in *The Original Series*, though its use was so blatant and heavy handed that you couldn't help but think, 'Why have they done that to her then? She must be a right old raddled hag in real life.'

TEN BABES FROM THE ORIGINAL SERIES* (BUT JUST THINK WHAT THEY'RE LIKE NOW)

1: Grace Lee Whitney. Janice Rand was included mainly to be decorative, at which she was undeniably talented, and to provide some romantic interest for Kirk (yeah, like one woman would be enough). Her all-too-brief appearances were so insubstantial that it wasn't until 'Flashback' that we discovered the true extent of her acting ability.

2: Mariette Hartley. As well as playing Zarabeth, she also turned up in one of those Roddenberry-conceived, post-apocalypse TV movies that all merge into one in the memory. Having conquered the belly button-exposing taboo in *TOS* (see BUTTONS, BELLY), Gene decided to go one better for this (no, not those) – he gave Mariette's character two navels. Woo, kinkee! In denoting strange alienness, however, this was quite an improvement on lumpy foreheads.

3: Yvonne Craig played nutcase Marta in a skimpy outfit in 'Whom Gods Destroy'. Never mind, if you find you can't perv over the erstwhile Batgirl anymore, there's always Alicia Silverstone.

4: Dyanne Thorne didn't have a great deal to do in 'A Piece Of The Action' but later in her career she saw plenty of action in *Ilsa, She-wolf of the SS* and its sequels *Ilsa, Harem Keeper of the Sheiks* and *Ilsa, The Wicked Warden*. Classics all.

5: Sherry Jackson was Andrea in 'What are Little Girls Made Of?' and wore one of those *TOS* costumes famous for showing flesh in unusual places and thus appearing to be more revealing than they actually are. If only she'd worn it back to front.

6: Barbara Bouchet. Although she is best remembered by *Star Trek* fans for her appearance in 'By Any Other Name' playing Kelinda, it is generally forgotten that she once played Miss Moneypenny in a James Bond film. Though, as the Bond film was *Casino Royale*, that's probably a good thing.

7: Susan Denberg. She was a babe and a half, even by Harry Mudd's standards. Pity then she took the saying 'Die young, stay pretty' so literally.

8: Terri Garr. Actually, she still looks great so she must have been about nine or something when she did 'Assignment: Earth'. She's often credited as Terry Garr – he's probably her brother.

9: France Nuyen. Actually, she wasn't really our type, but she played Elaan of Troyius and we wanted to get in a line about her having a face that launched a thousand starships. (Though was it really worth it?)

10: Anjelique Pettyjohn. We're lost for words.

* It goes without saying that Majel Barrett would top our list, but we wanted to give someone else a chance.**

** This applies to Nichelle Nichols too. By the way, have you ever seen those nudie shots? Nichelle has denied they were her, and we wouldn't dream of disputing her claim. But it has to be said that if the person in the pics ever turned up at a Star Trek convention, she'd win the Uhura-lookalike contest no problem.

FORBIDDEN PLANET: Classic '50s SF movie with Leslie Nielsen as the heroic starship captain and Robbie the Robot as his logical right-hand, erm, robot. We'd swear that the set-up was really quite similar to *Star Trek*'s, if only we weren't 100% positive that Gene Roddenberry's concept was completely original.

'FOR THE WORLD IS HOLLOW AND I HAVE TOUCHED THE SKY': Honestly, what were they on when they chose episode titles for season three of *The Original Series*? Other such pretentious gems include 'And the Children Shall Lead', 'Is There in Truth No Beauty?' and 'Let That Be Your Last Battlefield'. Far more poetic than the actual scripts, we think.

'FOUR BEGINNINGS, THE': Boxed set of *Star Trek* videos featuring four series pilots. By this point, do we really have to point out that there are five beginnings?

FOUR LIGHTS: Picard probably thought he was being dead heroic and all by resisting Cardassian attempts to persuade him that he was looking at five lights and not four in 'Chain of Command'. But really, what was the point in allowing himself to be tortured like that? If they'd been trying to extract vital Federation secrets, then fair enough, but the exact number of bulbs in the room can't have been of much consequence, and surely the Cardassians could have counted for themselves if it was. Take heed: if you do find yourself in such a situation, the application of a little common sense is all that's required. Just spare yourself a lot of pain by saying, 'Yes, there are five lights. Absolutely.' Once your crew has rescued you, as they are bound to do, you can wave two fingers at your erstwhile captors and say, 'Ha ha, I was lying all along.' They'll be so cross.

FRAME-TRAY JIGSAW PUZZLE: What exactly a frame-tray jigsaw puzzle is, we're not sure. What we do know about the one we found at a local jumble sale, however, is: it was produced by Whitman; it has a picture on it of someone in a space suit who could well be Captain Kirk; it has at least ten pieces; it helps co-ordination and motor control. Admittedly some Trekkies are a bit geeky, but that last bit is a tad insulting.

FRANCHISE, THE *TREK*: Term coined by Paramount to describe *Star Trek* in its entirety, presumably because they associate it less with the provision of quality entertainment and more with the accumulation of great wodges of cash. Even so, it is interesting to note that the word 'franchise' is used here to mean something completely dissimilar to any of its dictionary definitions.

FRANKLIN MINT: Purveyors of such fine quality *Star Trek* merchandise as chess sets and precious metal replicas of various insignias and emblems. Items without which the lives of all devoted Trekkies would be all the poorer. Except in the financial sense of the word obviously.

FRASIER: In a TV celebration of all things *Star Trek*, actors from this show appeared alongside Kate Mulgrew in a *Voyager* sketch (though the ill-informed caption writers seemed to think it was *DS9*). In retrospect it probably wasn't a good idea to use such likeable and popular characters, as unfair comparisons were bound to follow. On the plus side, however, there is now one enjoyable, if a little short, *Voyager* episode.

TEN VERSIONS OF *STAR TREK* THAT WE ALMOST GOT TO SEE

1: The *Frasier* episode lost its star when Kelsey Grammer checked himself into the Betty Ford clinic. Which is just as well, as fans would no doubt have assumed he was Captain Bateson from 'Cause and Effect'. Kate Mulgrew became *Voyager*'s last-minute replacement captain for the second time.

2: DeForest Kelley was originally offered the role of a green-skinned Spock, but turned it down. Leonard Nimoy got out of wearing the green paint, but was given a stupid pair of stuck-on pointy ears instead.

3: *The Next Generation* almost went ahead without a precocious teenage boy in its cast. Nope, it would have had a precocious teenage girl instead, by the name of Leslie Crusher. Of course, they had to change it: how would they have paid homage to the great Gene Roddenberry otherwise (see EUGENE)?

4: *Voyager* almost starred Nicholas Locarno, from the *Next Gen* episode 'First Duty'. Locarno was a temperamental young officer with a dubious track record, played by Robert Duncan McNeill. Instead we got Tom Paris, a temperamental young officer with a dubious track record, played by Robert Duncan McNeill. So why not Locarno? Seems they thought he was too far beyond redemption and could never have grown into a perfect American hero as Paris has.

5: Julian Bashir almost jumped ship (well, station) to serve on *Voyager* – where he might have been accompanied by Reg Barclay (Dwight Schultz guest-starred as a hologram instead).

6: Robert Picardo was considered for the role of Neelix, and was disappointed to become the holographic doctor instead, as he felt that the part was less interesting. Ah, the things we can know with hindsight . . .

7: Tim Russ was short listed for the part of Geordi LaForge. As Tuvok, he probably appears more frequently, but only to get knocked about and beaten up.

8: The Bajoran ensign Ro was to have transferred across to *DS9* with Miles O'Brien, but Michelle Forbes chose not to go. They created Major Kira instead, a character who is . . . well, not so different really.

9: Denise Crosby and Marina Sirtis swapped their *Next Gen* roles on the first day of filming, so Tasha Yar would presumably still be alive had they not, whilst Deanna Troi would have been blasted to atoms. Hmm, this has a strange sort of appeal.

10: Max Grodenchik was down to the last two actors considered to play Quark, but was asked back to be Rom instead. Still, all those Ferengi look alike to us.

———◆———

FRIEBURGER, FRED: Producer brought in for the third and, as it turned out, final series of *Star Trek: The Original Series*, and we all remember how good that was. Long-time puppet supremo Gerry Anderson was suitably impressed, however. When he finally realised that his live-action characters had significantly less in the way of personality than his super marionettes, he enlisted the services of Frieburger, who produced the second and, as it turned out, final series of *Space: 1999*.

FRIENDS: OK, so nothing's ever completely black and white (not even 'The Cage'), but why is it that no major antagonist in *Star Trek* can stay bad for too long? First it was the Klingons: there we all were thinking what a nasty lot of dirty-faced, bearded gits they were, when all the time they were really just a misunderstood race of noble warriors. Then came the Ferengi. From the outset, they were never really serious contenders for the vacated spot of main *Trek* villains, being more inclined to sell you a used spaceship than to cut off your head with a bat'leth – so no surprise then when we ended up with a lovable bartender, never mind Starfleet wannabe Nog. The Cardassians had potential, but once they were firmly established as part of the *Trek* universe, redemption was close at hand. Take Garak for instance: as a former member of the Obsidian Order, he could easily have had an unsavoury past full of torture and brutality, yet he virtually comes across as John Steed with a lumpy head. And we won't even mention Dukat's daughter. Showing the most promise of all were that race of drug-crazed violent psychopaths the Jem'Hadar – mad bastards and no mistake. Then along came a nice one who wanted Doctor Bashir to help them overcome their addiction and free them from dependence on their shape-shifting masters (who are no doubt about to change their ways and throw a big party). Finally, of all the opponents to have faced the various *Enterprise*s and other franchise off-shoots, surely the Borg were the most worthy. And, bearing the above in mind, the escapade with Hugh Borg was inevitable and could really be regarded as an interesting slant on the Borg lifestyle or even a fair swap for Locutus. However, the last thing we expected was for one of the Borg collective to become a *Star Trek* regular: not even *Voyager* could entertain such a dumb idea. Could it? Well, yes, it seems it could. The bad news: Kes leaves *Voyager* and is replaced by a female Borg (*Dark Skies'* Jeri Lynn Ryan, who we hope is better at Borgs than Russians). The good news: with Kes out of the show, there's no point in watching it any more. Who needs to see Janeway fretting about that nasty, Borg-beating new alien race anyway, when in a few years' time she'll be lying in bed next to one of them and a few long-dead red-shirts won't matter a jot.

FRONT EAR, FINAL: Weak punchline to a feeble gag about the number of ears Captain Kirk has (three). The one good thing about this joke is that Trekkies can personally tailor it by substituting their own favourite character for Kirk. However, if telling it in the company of non-fans, it is better to avoid obscure people and stick to popular figures like Mr Spock and Jean-Luc Picard. Though of course, it still won't get a laugh. There's also a video by this name available, in which stand-up comedian George Marshall performs *Star Trek* material for an audience of fans. We can't comment further as we haven't seen it: we're too worried that, were the contents to be as hilarious as its title, we would be unable to survive the 50-odd minutes of organ-rupturing mirth.

TEN COMMONLY USED *STAR TREK* JOKES THAT ARE, IN FACT, CRAP AND OBVIOUS

1: OK, so the opening titles of both *The Original Series* and *The Next Generation* feature the words 'to boldly go', right? Well, by the cunning substitution of just one vowel, you can make this 'to baldly go', which is really quite funny. It can apply to several characters too, which gives it lots of potential for repeated use. And don't even think about how the cast of the first six movies might 'oldly go' – you could do yourself a mischief.

2: Klingons, eh? Wahey, sounds a bit like cling-ons, doesn't it lads? Not that cling-ons is actually a real slang term – but if it was, it would surely mean something scatological. Chortle!

3: And Klingons' foreheads look just like ... well actually, there's a choice here. See QUCH for more details.

4: Here's a great tip for current affairs shows: start every *Star Trek* feature with a shot of the presenter beaming into the studio. This will be extremely amusing and totally unexpected.

5: And if he's wearing a ludicrous pair of comedy Spock-ears too, you're guaranteed to have an audience in stitches.

6: You know that Geordi LaForge? Well he's not a real Geordie, is he? (UK only.)

7: What's more, the *Original Star Trek* communicator looks a bit like a lady's powder compact, so the sight of someone in Starfleet uniform (or a close approximation) flipping one of these open to reveal a mirror and some make-up will always raise a cheap laugh (from the sketch writer).

8: Likewise, stardates offer endless potential for humour. For example: 'Captain's log, stardate February.' Ha ha ha.

9: But for a really good guffaw, you'll want the *Enterprise* crew to be unable to string a sentence together without using clichés. So Spock has to make lots of logical assumptions, the hailing frequencies must always be open, the engines willnae be able to take it and, dammit, McCoy is a doctor. The problem with this one is that *The Original Series* did it already.

10: For an encore, dress your aliens up in cheap tin foil and let strings appear in your model shots. In fact, this is such a great gag that it works for every SF show going. Yes, that's really fair isn't it? Let's deride anyone who tries to create something imaginative, so that programme controllers will be embarrassed into producing more low-budget soap operas and game shows instead.

G

GALILEO: Apparently this is the *Enterprise*'s seventh shuttle craft, but it gets a lot more use than any of the others – it even got its own episode once. Sadly it got destroyed in this, but was soon resurrected. We don't know why this should be, unless it's to save painting another name and number on the full-size shuttle craft prop.*

* And before the pedantry starts, the reason we didn't mention that it had 'Galileo II' painted on it when it landed on Eden is that it would have made the numbering system even more difficult to follow. And anyway, before you start getting too cocky, what about when it doubled for that shuttle craft stolen from Starbase 4 by Lokai eh?

GARTH, LORD, MASTER OF THE UNIVERSE: Escaped loony whose cellular metamorphosis into Captain Kirk allowed William Shatner an opportunity like never before to go completely over the top. He did not disappoint, and in particular his temper tantrum is a joy to behold, surpassing even the maniacal laughter.

GENETRON: Interesting sounding machine featured in *Voyager* that sadly turned out not to be a development of the Orgasmatron as seen in *Barbarella*, but was instead something to do with genetics. Dunno what, we lost interest at that point.

'GET A LIFE!': Immortal phrase uttered by William Shatner during a *Saturday Night Live* mock-up of a *Star Trek* convention in 1986. Plagued by insanely trivial questions from a (pretend) audience of fans, Shatner accused them of turning an 'enjoyable little job' into 'a colossal waste of time' before asking one if he had ever kissed a girl (he hadn't). The rebuke has now passed into common English usage, even in the UK where the episode in question was not shown (although clips have been transmitted). Fortunately for those fans who were upset by all this, Shatner's claim to have been possessed by Kirk's evil double at the time was entirely convincing.

'GIANT IN THE UNIVERSE': A thrilling three-dimensional adventure which, coming as it did in 1977, more than made up for the cancellation of *Star Trek II*. The *Enterprise* crew find a gigantic planet and, beaming down, come face to groin with a giant (hence the planet's size, presumably). The giant traps them in enormous glasses, which they dissolve with their phasers before beaming back up to the ship. Sheer brilliance! And, as if this pop-up book didn't provide enough nerve-jangling tension, Random House published another. It's called *Trillions of Trilligs*, so we daren't even open it.

GIDEON: Massively over-populated world. Its rulers were taking a bit of a risk therefore when they requested that Kirk be the one to beam down as the Federation's representative.

GOMEZ, SONYA: Over-enthusiastic Starfleet Academy graduate who blotted her copy book from the outset by spilling her hot chocolate over Picard and just generally behaving in a naff manner. Which was appropriate really, because, funnily enough, she was played by Lycia Naff.

GORN: First-rate reptilian alien featured in 'Arena'; it's much harder than a Klingon and actually looks like it might come from another planet. Once again, it took *The Animated Series* to give this species another airing.

GREAT BIRD OF THE GALAXY, THE: Popular and enduring sobriquet dubbed upon Gene Roddenberry by *TOS* producer Bob Justman, and taken from a line in 'The Man Trap'. Trouble is, said line originally referred to Janice Rand

– and, even without that titbit of knowledge, Justman's idea of what typifies 'a great bird' appears to be at some variance with ours. The *Next Gen* team did their best to scotch, once and for all, the salacious image of Roddenberry having a great big pendulous pair of breasts, by super-imposing his face over a parrot's body and sticking the resultant picture into Starfleet records ('The Naked Now'). But, hey, who would have noticed that?*

* Not us, that's for sure – we read it somewhere.

GREEN BODY PAINT: This, it seems, is very sexy in the 23rd century, particularly when slapped all over nubile Orion dancing girls. Mr Spock, however, not wishing to appear too blatantly sensual, preferred the subtler approach with the application of just a touch of green eye shadow. How Kirk could keep his hands off we'll never know.

'GUILTY AS CHARGED': Kirk's verdict upon Spock when he stood trial in 'The Menagerie'. Had the Talosians not intervened, this would have led to Spock being executed. Well, that's what friends are for. We did have it in mind to produce a list of telling Kirk-isms; however, as this would have meant sitting through many tedious *TOS* episodes, we didn't bother. Suffice it to say, though, that it would have included such gems as 'I won't hurt you' (belated words of comfort to Akuta, a big jessie with a platinum-blond wig and heavy eye make-up, just after he's punched him in the face and made him cry) and 'I guess we weren't sufficiently entertaining' (a startling premonition of things to come, from the final season).

GUINAN: Whoopi Goldberg's semi-regular role as a mysterious bartender in *The Next Generation*. Critics might say that Guinan's sympathetic ear and skill with personal problems rendered Troi completely useless – but they'd be forgetting that Troi was completely useless to start with. Makes sense to us that, when your ship's counsellor is likely to respond to a suicide threat with a considered line like 'Hmmm, yes, I am

sensing a bit of depression' (see STATING THE BLEEDIN'
OBVIOUS), it's the woman who holds the key to the nearest
source of alcoholic oblivion who'll have to pick up the slack.

GUINEVERE: Presumably this was the holodeck persona
Kira had adopted when she punched out Lancelot for kissing
her; she was playing a married woman, after all.

HAIRPIECE: What the networks apparently wanted Patrick Stewart to wear in *The Next Generation*, as they still patronised American viewers to the extent that they thought a bald character might put them off the show. He tried it, but it looked crap. And may we just say that the idea of a captain of the USS *Enterprise* wearing such an accessory is not only ludicrous but completely and totally unprecedented. How could they have thought of such a thing?

HAMILTON COLLECTION, THE: Fairly recent addition to the long queue of companies who want to extort money, and lots of it, from Trekkies. Their lines of plates featuring *Star Trek* artwork are all well and good, but it is their rather immodest adverts which have endeared them to fandom. Their plates are 'compelling' and at least one of their artists is a 'genius'. Of their *Star Trek: The Movies* series, they boast: 'Now, for the first time ever, collectors can re-live the gripping drama of each of the *Star Trek* motion pictures.' Quite right. Who needs the videos when you can have the porcelain discs?

HANDS: Once used by Spock in an unsuccessful attempt to prevent a gaseous entity from entering a room through a ventilation grille. Not very logical that, was it?

HARRIMAN, JOHN: Kirk's successor as the Captain of the USS *Enterprise*, and not exactly an inspired choice to take over the Federation's flagship. Unless, of course, his job description simply read: 'Make Kirk look good, the flabby old git needs it.' Even if it did, he made a bit of a *faux pas* by getting his predecessor killed.

HEADSCARVES: In the universe of the 24th century, these innocuous items of clothing have found an unanticipated use as alien disguises. And very effective they are too. Great big unsightly brown lump on your head? No problem: just wrap a length of wool about it and no one will ever know. Hopefully Starfleet have cottoned* on to the insidious potential of this ruse by now, else the Klingons, et al., could all too easily infiltrate human society by simply sending their representatives to a hat-wearers' convention.

* *Cottoned, get it?*

HEINEKEN: Lager which, it is claimed, refreshes the parts other beers cannot reach. These parts included Mr Spock's ears, which appeared limp in a mid-'70s poster campaign but were soon standing proudly erect after a pint. We can understand why Captain Kirk wasn't chosen for the ad, as the most obvious part of his anatomy to be in need of refreshment would have got the posters banned. However, Leonard Nimoy was reportedly not amused (so perfectly in character, then).

HERBERT: Offensive futuristic term of abuse favoured by Starfleet Academy drop-outs and the like, and presumably the closest thing to an expletive the over-sensitive studio executives would allow. (See IDIOTS.)

HESKELL: Short-lived (literally) character in *TNG*'s 'Where Silence has Lease'. 'Hmm,' thinks Nagilum, the odd-looking cosmic entity the *Enterprise* has just encountered in a phenomenon a bit like the ship-eating, black emptiness thing of Klingon myth, 'I'll just kill one of the crew to see what it's like. But which one? Picard? No. Data? Don't think so. Riker? Tempting, but no. Hang on, who's that bloke in red sitting at the helm? He'll do.' (See also DEATH SEAT.)

'HIGHLY ILLOGICAL': In our opinion, it was highly illogical of the record company to bring out this compilation album of unforgettable (for all the wrong reasons) songs by Leonard Nimoy, for instance: 'The Ballad of Bilbo Baggins', 'If I had a Hammer' (if we had one we'd use it on this record) and a couple of Spock-based tracks so the fans'll buy it. Even more illogical though, to release 'The Transformed Man' on which William Shatner 'sings' fab tunes like 'Lucy in the Sky with Diamonds' and, erm 'Hamlet'. Give us 'Star Trekkin'' by The Firm any day.

THE *STAR TREK* TOP TEN

10: If you've always wanted to get down and groove to the *Voyager* theme, there's nothing left to stop you. Two funky, re-mixed pop versions are available on one fab CD single. Are you dancin'?

9: Or you can get several covers of '50s songs for the price of . . . erm, several, with 'Ol' Yellow Eyes is Back' by Brent Spiner and the Sunspots. The 'spots in question are Jonathan Frakes, LeVar Burton, Michael Dorn and Patrick Stewart, and they can almost sing in tune too.

8: 'William Shatner – Live!' Shatner can't almost sing in tune, so this is only good for a laugh (and the joke wears off after a couple of notes). It's also available under the name 'Captain of the Starship', not to suggest that the music isn't good enough to sell without bringing Kirk into it.

7: 'Leonard Nimoy Presents Mr Spock's Music from Outer Space'. Oh wow, don't you just have to rush out and buy this? No? Well, at least the single from the album – 'Visit to a Sad Planet' – sounds more descriptive of what it is.

6: 'Whales Alive'. Nimoy must have learned his lesson as, on this one, he just narrates and leaves the singing to a chorus of whales (which are about as melodious as he is). Nimoy is well used to working with scene-stealing, near-extinct, blubbery, hairless mammals from his association with the *Star Trek* films. Well, with *Star Trek IV* anyway (why, what did you think we meant?).

5: 'Disco Trekin' '. Grace Lee Whitney makes the first of her lesser-known entrées into the world of *Star Trek* on vinyl, with this up-beat number. If only it had been her last.

4: 'Beyond Antares/Uhura's Theme'. Nichelle Nichols re-records a couple of Uhura's little ditties from the series and proves to be . . . well, actually, quite good.

3: *Star Trek: The Motion Picture* soundtrack. You really can't appreciate this film until you've heard it unfettered by the rather disappointing plot, sets, dialogue, costumes, effects, etc. We mean it.

2: 'The *Star Trek* Philosophy'. To orchestral accompaniment, Gene Roddenberry expounds upon the details of his utopian future. 'Nuff said.

1: 'Star Trekkin' ' by The Firm, presumably taking a leaf out of Grace Lee's book. This actually reached the number one slot in the UK, but then bizarre things do sometimes happen. We would slag it off, but we don't really want to be known as a big pair of Firm knockers.

HILL, DIXON: Holodeck persona of Jean-Luc Picard. You'd think he'd have more than enough real-life excitement fighting the Borg and stuff without having to pretend to be a pulp magazine sleuth to get his kicks. It just goes to show that, although war and poverty will be eliminated by the 24th century, the character traits that go to make up the sort of sad losers who get off on Dungeons and Dragons-type role-playing games will still be inherent.

HODGKIN'S LAW OF PARALLEL PLANET DEVELOPMENT: Sometimes you wonder why they ever bothered boldly going to seek out new life and new civilisations when most of the places where they ended up seemed a lot like the one they'd set out from, in various stages of its development – Beta III, for instance, a planet populated entirely by extras from an episode of *Gunsmoke*. Hodgkin's law was an unsatisfactory explanation for the proliferation of uncomfortably Earth-like worlds in the galaxy, but a bloody-good excuse for re-using any job lot of old movie costumes that happened to be lying around the Paramount studios. Later on, to justify the fact that most life forms in the *Star Trek* universe are humanoid, albeit with various facial bumps, there was all that rubbish in *Next Gen* about one race of aliens seeding the Galaxy in its own image.* This sort of thing, of course, is just thrown out to the fans as ammunition against non-Trekkies: any criticisms can now be answered with a rather smug, 'Ah, but they explained all that in 'The Chase', so there!' It does them no good in the long run, though. Far better, in our opinion, to make such people face up to reality. So here goes . . . IT'S ONLY A TELEVISION PROGRAMME, AND ALL THOSE SO-CALLED ALIENS ARE REALLY MEN IN SUITS. Yes, we know it hurts, but you'll thank us for it one day.

* *Perhaps, one day, we'll also learn that a race of interior designers, with a fetish for certain types of rock, decorated hundreds of planets, a few aeons ago.*

HOLODECK: Totally unfeasible piece of technology introduced in *The Next Generation* (from an idea in *The Animated Series*), but certainly the sort of thing that someone should be working towards merchandising, rather than fake phasers, Mr Spock teddies and the like. Our objection to it (apart from the increasingly worn, 'Oh look, we were on the holodeck all along!' plot cop-out) is that everyone seems to use the amenity in such an unrealistic way. Come on, if such a thing had malfunctioned and merged all its programs into real life as it did in 'Emergence', the *Enterprise* crew would hardly have been confronted by train conductors, knights and hitmen, now would they? No, they'd have been knee deep in whip-wielding dominatrixes, bronzed muscleman-types, blond life-guards and sheep. Mind you, as Picard can – and does – walk onto the deck whenever he feels like it, perhaps his crew have to be a bit careful with their fantasies. As usual, it's left to *Deep Space Nine* to add a touch of credibility, and indeed the holosuites in Quark's Bar are strongly hinted to be no more than technological knocking shops. The episode in which they break down and scatter their characters across the station has, oddly, yet to be written.

HOMOSEXUALITY: *Star Trek* has dedicated itself to the creation of an enlightened future in which all human prejudices have been eradicated. In a series of ground-breaking moves which have inspired shock and admiration in the American public, even women and black people have been allowed to have careers. So what taboos are left? Well, once its creator was out of the way, the franchise was able to begin an exploration of homosexuality in a number of thought-provoking episodes. For example, how does Picard react when pursued by an alien woman who turns out to be a sex-changing ambassador? Should the fact that a Trill is given a new, female, host alter Doctor Crusher's love for the person beneath the skin (and there was that similar storyline with Dax too)? And, arriving on a world with an androgynous population, does Riker's Kirk-like image require that he bonk at least one of them? Yes indeedy, *Star Trek* has now done everything it can to promote acceptance and understanding of those with alternative lifestyles. Well, apart from featuring a gay character of course, 'cos that would just be disgusting.

HORNS: Often used to turn what would otherwise be less-than-terrifying creatures into formidable adversaries for Kirk* and friends. Take the Mugato, for example: a fluffy, white gorilla-type-of-thing, and quite the cutest ape since the son of Kong capered amusingly across our screens,** but stick a big horn in the middle of its head and . . . oh crikey, that's sooo scary!

He's quite horny too, but that's another thing entirely.
** *And obviously quite keen to make a polite impression too, hence its eschewing of its usual naked state to appear in a smart dress uniform for the release of its inevitable action figure.*

HORSE IMPRESSION, KIRK'S: No, on second thoughts, we won't embarrass our readers by mentioning it.

HORTA: A silicon-based life form (i.e., a comedy rock). Given the sheer number of rocks in *The Original Series* (see ROCKS), it was perhaps only a matter of time before we encountered an intelligent one. Indeed, one might almost suspect that she had been following Kirk and company around from world to world, just waiting for a chance to start something. The Horta told Spock that she found the appearance of humans revolting, which almost makes her eligible to join that most exclusive club comprised of females who don't fancy Captain Kirk. But, despite giving him a stony-faced reception, she did spare his life when – given his track record – the most sensible thing would have been to get in there first. Perhaps she was beginning to crumble beneath his charm offensive?

HUDDERSFIELD FC: Football team supported by Patrick Stewart. What other *Star Trek* reference work gives you crucial information like that, eh?

HUMOUR: If Data is keen to continue the development of his sense of humour, he would be well advised not to pay too close attention to suggestions from his fellow crewmates. The whole po-faced lot of them reckoned that pushing Doctor Crusher into the water (in *Generations*) was not at all amusing, when in fact it was very funny indeed.

HYBRIDS: Tuvok put a lot of effort into creating one of these with a South American orchid and a Vulcan plant, and was surprised that it actually worked. He can't have been paying much attention, then. What did he think half the members of Starfleet were, let alone his ship's own head of engineering? Hybrid characters seem to have become the inevitable final stage in the customary transition of *Trek* aliens from aggressors to sympathetic characters to regulars in the next off-shoot to spreading their seeds (see FRIENDS). So long as alien plants are even half as adept at interbreeding, Tuvok couldn't have had an easier task if he'd just tried to get two compatible orchids to cross-pollinate (or whatever it is that flowers get up to).

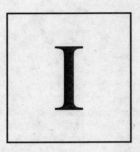

I AM NOT SPOCK: The title of Leonard Nimoy's first autobiography, published in 1975, which echoed his resentment at being typecast as a cold-blooded Vulcan science officer from the future. Understandable really, as that sort of role doesn't come up too often. This attitude, though, was an easy target for ridicule, and so it was that the topical, satirical *Spitting Image* laid into it only ten years later. They made a latex puppet of Nimoy – complete with floppy ears – and had it vainly protest its ability as a serious actor, as a running (i.e., oft-repeated) gag for a couple of series. Presumably Nimoy got the message, as he later cited the book's title as his biggest regret in life and released a sequel volume called *I Am Spock*. As we all thought, really.

I AM SPOCK: Wish he'd just make his mind up. The most noteworthy aspect of this sequel volume is Nimoy's revelation that he conducts conversations with his half-Vulcan character in his head. Hmm, perhaps he should have kept quiet about that.

ICONIANS: Legendary race from the distant past whose technology was so advanced it seemed akin to magic. Picard saw to it that these wonderful achievements didn't fall into Romulan hands by simply shutting the door. No wonder he made captain.

IDIOTS: Grossly offensive expletive that NBC's Broadcast Standards Department once insisted upon removing from a *Star Trek* script. What a bunch of id**ts.

'I'M A DOCTOR, NOT AN ESCALATOR': McCoy's best variation on a theme. And isn't it funny that the holographic doctor has started to use this sort of line too? Some fans have claimed that he must have been partially programmed with McCoy's memories – but we think it's just the writers trying to be funny and desperately hoping to get some *TOS* fans to like *Voyager*.

IMPRESSION, KIRK'S HORSE: You know, it really is tempting to go on at great length about this. But it just wouldn't be possible to write anything that is half as amusing as the scene in question. Besides which, the mere reminder of it could put *Star Trek* fans off the series for life, and we can't be responsible for that. So, all things considered, we'll give it a miss.

INFINITIVE, SPLIT: Who is going to seriously give a toss?

INTERGALACTIC CHEERLEADER: What Counsellor Troi resembled in the first season of *The Next Generation*, according to Rick Berman. Well, as she had no other obvious use, why didn't they just go for it? Much as the New Zealand rugby team have their hakka to intimidate opponents, and the Klingons . . . well, they have all sorts of interminably dull rituals, don't they? . . . Deanna could have beamed down to planets with her crewmates and disoriented potential enemies by dancing up and down nearby, shouting '1-7-0-1! Who do we want to have won?' Or something. In the event, Troi's costume was changed after season one to something more dignified (plenty of choice there, then), thus bringing to a close the long-standing tradition that *Star Trek* women should be used primarily as set decoration (see BUTTONS, BELLY). We don't accept this was necessary, ourselves: after all, no matter how revealing Deanna's one-piece mini might have been, we never actually saw her pompoms.

INTERNET: Electronic system of communication which runs several forums for *Star Trek* fans; in fact, *SFX* once estimated that 20% of all traffic on the world-wide web consisted of people visiting *Star Trek* sites. Why doesn't this surprise us? If you want to while away a boring hour, morning or lifetime discussing why *Voyager* and *Deep Space Nine* are crap* and *The Original Series* reigns supreme, or whether a Galaxy Class Starship could batter a Death Star from *Star Wars*,** then this is the virtual place for you. On the plus side, we learnt far more about the series from postings on the web than from every issue of *TV Zone* put together – and some of the insults were quite fun too.

Although there's still talk of a letter-writing campaign to stop the latter being cancelled after it has run its course of six seasons. It is Star Trek, after all.

** *We may have inadvertently made this seem a bit interesting; however, by the time you've waded through page after page after page of technobabble, a truer picture will emerge. Much as we'd like to, we can't take credit for the very sensible suggestion that they just forget the hardware and have Kirk take on Jabba the Hutt in a belly-flop contest.*

IN THE NAVY: If Cardassian military commanders are called Guls, does that make their naval equivalents Sea Guls?

IN VINO VERITAS: As if *The Animated Series* wasn't enough to sustain even the most fervent Trekkie through the '70s, New Jersey-based Power Records released this audio-only adventure in which a host of anonymous actors did their utmost to recreate such well-loved *Trek* characters as Kirk, Spock, McCoy, Scotty and Transporter Chief Kyle (Uhura is mentioned, but presumably none of the all-male cast could manage her voice – though their shortcomings in the mimicry department didn't otherwise hold them back). Kirk and Spock are the Federation's representatives at a conference to resolve a dispute over the proprietary rights to a planet. Also attending are ambassadors from the Klingon Empire and, er, Romula. A spanner is thrown into the works when the notorious Coriolanus Quince spikes the wine with a drug that causes all the delegates to speak nothing but the complete truth, thus rendering the diplomatic process imposs-ible (little bit o' politics there). Several more of these 'little

LPs' were produced, but we couldn't find the others in the discount store.

IRISH UNIFICATION OF 2024: If this doesn't happen, it's really going to blow *Star Trek*'s credibility. Perhaps that's why the UK censors saw fit to spare the producers' blushes by cutting the offending line. While we're thinking about it, there had better be 52 American states by 2033 too.

ISS *ENTERPRISE* – NCC 1701: Mirror universe starship that is, as you might expect, pretty similar to the USS *Enterprise* – NCC 1701. Nevertheless, the *Star Trek Fact Files* thought it deserving of a blueprint of its very own. Oh hang on, here's a different bit: there's a letter I on the saucer section instead of a U. Worth including it, then.

J

JACK THE RIPPER: Long-lived telefantasy series regular (he was in *Babylon 5* too) responsible for a series of brutal murders on the fog-shrouded brothel of a planet Argelius II. Or was he? We suspect he was in fact the innocent victim of an insidious cover-up perpetrated by Kirk and his cronies, in a vile attempt to hide the true identity of the killer – Mr Scott. The evidence is clear for all to see: Scotty, suffering from a blow to the head which has made him resent women (well, that's what scriptwriter Robert Bloch implied) is discovered on three separate occasions covered in blood, knife in hand, standing over the recently butchered corpse of a young woman. A bit more than circumstantial, wouldn't you say? So what does Kirk do after the first murder? Does he put Scotty safely under lock and key, away from further temptation? No, he leaves him alone with the second victim while he himself tries to implicate the father and fiancé of the first. Then, the normally trustworthy Spock becomes embroiled in the deceit: in a flagrant breach of the Prime Directive he attempts to avoid having Scotty undergo the Argelian process of justice in favour of the *Enterprise*'s own so-called foolproof system, which ultimately proves to be anything but. Back on the *Enterprise*, the most far-fetched tale imaginable is concocted. Based on pure guesswork, Kirk, McCoy and the rest claim that the murderer is Jack the Ripper, who's actually a malevolent gaseous entity. What makes this all the more suspicious is the fact that the *Enterprise* had encountered a malevolent gaseous entity in only the week before's episode, so the idea was obviously still fresh in their minds. Now with some of the heat off Scotty, the planet's off-world administrator Hengist is accused, despite there being only the flimsiest of incriminating evidence – the murder weapon originated on the same planet as him. And he confesses! Come on, as if the real Jack the Ripper would have evaded capture for centuries if he'd broken down and confessed every time someone pointed an accusing finger!

'Excuse me, sir, but did you 'appen to 'orribly mutilate this 'ere dead tart?'

'No, officer, I'm afraid I can't help you there.'

'Sorry to trouble you then, sir. Good evening.'

Most likely, Hengist's confession was the result of skil-fully administered drugs and hypnosis (implicating McCoy, and suggesting Spock's involvement went even deeper) and part of the same elaborate ploy to extricate Scotty which then saw the ship's computers programmed to appear as if under the control of some evil disembodied force. We'll probably never know the full story behind the murders as a fair trial was ruled out when Hengist was swiftly bundled into a transporter and his atoms scattered across deep space. Fortunately, it seems the chief engineer recovered from the bump on the head and was never tempted to kill again; even so, he was never punished for his evil crimes and remained, erm, scot-free.

JANEWAY, KATHRYN: Starfleet captain seemingly capable of only two poses lest she ruffle her immaculate hair. When it was rumoured that Kate Mulgrew was leaving *Voyager* and that her character was to be killed off in battle,* some fans unkindly remarked on the fact that her repertoire doesn't include a duck-ing position.

* *Did you know, by the way, that this rumour was started by a group of West Midland fanboys to test how gullible the internet discussion groups were? Well you do now. We'd like to claim that we never believed a word of it at the time, but in fact it would be more accurate to say that we just didn't care.*

JANSSEN, FAMKE: Eponymous guest star of *TNG*'s 'The Perfect Mate'. No arguments from us about that particular piece of casting.

JASON OF STAR COMMAND: A must for all real fans of *Star Trek*. Not only does this mid-'70s science fiction series star Jimmy Doohan (who, of course, provided voices for *The Animated Series*) as Commander Canarvin, it was also produced by Filmation, of *The Animated Series* fame, and thus boasts the exact same incidental score that was used in *The Animated Series*, and in fact every other Filmation cartoon of the time. Come to think of it, the quality of the special effects, scenery, acting, costumes, etc., made *Jason of Star Command* look just like *The Animated Series* too. And what's more, some of it was written by Samuel A Peeples, who scripted *The Animated Series*'s pilot episode (oh, and the pilot of another early version of *Star Trek* too). Since *The Animated Series* never made it to a third season, this can be considered a replacement of sorts. Well, it could, but for one rather unfortunate fact: it's total crap.

TEN GREAT PLACES TO FIND *STAR TREK* ACTORS*

1: Kate Mulgrew played 'er indoors, who was alluded to but never seen in *Columbo*, but who graduated to her own series, none the less, as *Mrs Columbo*. *Columbo*'s producers objected to this, and the link was dropped when the series returned as *Kate Loves a Mystery*. Perhaps Kate has a memory block, as she only seems able to play characters who share her christian name. Even Kathryn Janeway was Elizabeth Janeway when Genevieve Bujold had the role.

2: LeVar Burton shot to fame in *Roots* which, coincidentally, coined the term 'The Next Generation' for its second series (the one he wasn't in). *Roots* broke all audience records in the States, but was far more notable for having LeVar play a character called Kunta.

3: William Shatner did a couple of *Twilight Zones* and proved that he can act when he doesn't try too hard.

4: Marina Sirtis starred in a crap film remake (well, it was directed by Michael Winner) of *The Wicked Lady*, notable only for its inclusion of a lengthy scene featuring a topless Marina and a whip. Get it out now (no, we mean the video).

5: Terry Farrell played a very different Cat in *Red Dwarf USA*, when the networks hoped to cash in on the popularity of the British show by doing their own completely dissimilar version. There were two pilots (she was in the second), but both flopped (a bit like Terry herself, in *Off the Mark*). It's probably good news that *Red Dwarf USA* didn't get made, else she might not have been available for *DS9*; the downside is that we never got to see her pussy.

6: Leonard Nimoy appeared in the original series of *The Outer Limits* in the episode 'I, Robot', and he turned up in the revival series of *The Outer Limits* in the episode 'I, Robot'. Not many people can lay claim to that. Nimoy also became a regular in *Mission Impossible*, perhaps hoping he'd left *Star Trek* behind forever. Not so. His character was called Paris – which, as we all know now, is the name of the rugged, slightly flawed guy who keeps spreading his seed in *Voyager*.

7: Speaking of Paris, Robert Duncan McNeill starred in *Masters of the Universe*, a mirror image of *Star Trek* in that the series was based on an enormous range of action figures. So if Playmates/Bandai can't churn out those poseable crew models in every conceivable costume fast enough for you, just buy yourself a 'Tom Paris with huge rippling muscles and battle armour' figure. It's bound to come in useful.

8: Michael Pataki, sometime Klingon actor, was the crusty Captain Barbera in the cheesy '70s *Spider-Man* series. Doubtless this paved the way for Nichelle Nichols's villainous role in the recent cartoon version of the web-slinger's adventures: her second association with a classic animated series.

9: Dwight Schultz (Barclay) was Murdoch in *The A-Team*, famous in the UK for upsetting puritans with scenes of violence too gratuitous for its slot on kids' TV. Apparently, it was considered an adult show in America . . . But never mind that, Dwight was also in a 1996 remake of *Hart to Hart*!

10: Best of all, René Auberjonois voiced multiple guest stars over several years in *Scooby-Doo*. And he'd have gotten away with it too, if it hadn't been for those pesky kids.

As opposed to ten boring ones like T J Hooker, The Man From UNCLE *or Walter Koenig and Majel Barrett's roles in* Babylon 5.

JAZZED-UP THEME TUNE: What *Deep Space Nine* was given for its fourth season when someone realised that the original version didn't quite reach the heights of heart-stopping excitement to which it aspired. With a change in tempo, the addition of a not-at-all-appropriate backbeat (swiftly changed to a not-quite-appropriate one) and ships whooshing by à la *The Original Series*, it actually sounded quite ... well, quite like the old one really.

JEFFRIES TUBES: One of the most endearing features of the original *Enterprise*, these narrow claustrophobic vents allowed Chief Engineer Montgomery Scott to wriggle about the bowels of the ship carrying out his customary engineering miracles. They didn't seem to have them in the films, though; can't think why.

JELLO MAN: Fan nickname for Odo, though we can think of a few other characters to whom it could equally apply.

JOANNE: Dr McCoy's daughter. She was supposed to feature in *TOS* season three and, needless to say, Kirk would have swooped straight in on her, causing friction between him and his old friend. The idea was dropped, perhaps because of the change in producer – but there are no prizes for guessing that Joanne was introduced into *Star Trek* continuity after all, via a mention in *The Animated Series*.

JONES, DAVY: First choice to join the cosmopolitan crew of the *Enterprise* in *TOS* season two was a character who would emulate the popularity of the mop-topped Englishman, so adept at tambourine playing in *The Monkees*. However, the makers of *Star Trek* finally conceded that the Russians had also made some contribution to the space race – in that they got there first (which, admittedly, was a more significant contribution than that of *The Monkees*). A compromise was reached and we got a mop-topped young Russian. Chekov's tambourine playing skills, however, remain shrouded in mystery. (See also KEPTIN.)

JUNKIES: Research has revealed that 5–10% of *Star Trek* fans meet the psychological criteria of addiction, displaying similar symptoms to drug dependants. Not to worry however, Dr Sandy Wolfson says that being hooked on *Trek* is beneficial rather than harmful, due to the enrichment it provides in Trekkies' lives. Hmm, maybe so, but bear in mind that using cocaine could work out cheaper than collecting Franklin Mint's output.

K

KAHLESS: Legendary Klingon famed for his impressive weapon.

KAZON: Recurring Delta Quadrant foes of the *Voyager* crew. It would be unfair to label them second-rate imitations of the Klingons, because they are really nothing like them – well apart from their war-orientated culture and lumpy foreheads that is (though that could equally apply to 99.9% of the alien races in *Star Trek*). What does set the Kazon apart from the rest, however, is their penchant for tasteful knitwear and the ability to grow mushrooms on their heads.

KENSIT, PATSY: Early candidate for the role of *Voyager*'s captain. Hmm, what a commanding presence she'd have been. No doubt, though, there'd have been many subtle differences had this actress been cast: for example, her holodeck fantasies may not have been inspired so much by the works of Charlotte Brontë as by the *Guinness Book of British Hit Singles*.

TEN BRITISH ACTORS WHO ACTUALLY DID APPEAR IN *STAR TREK*

1: Malcolm McDowell. Now infamous in Trekkie circles for his portrayal of Doctor Sorin, the character responsible for the death of Captain Kirk. Surely that should be deserving of some kind of award?

2: Joan Collins. Her appearance in 'City on the Edge of Forever' led to such other great projects as *Dynasty* and, well, *The Stud* and *The Bitch*.

3: Rosalyn Landor. *C.A.T.S. Eyes* was never the same after she left.

4: Mick Fleetwood. Yeah, suppose we did say actors. But never mind, eh?

5: David Warner. Obviously this actor was regarded as one of the few good things about *Star Trek V*, as he was signed up to appear in *Star Trek VI*.

6: Maurice Roeves. One of the very few actors to have appeared in both *Star Trek* and *Doctor Who*. Hmm, that's almost interesting that is.

7: Barrie Ingham. He was in the first film version of *Doctor Who*, which is even less interesting.

8: Judy Geeson. Playing a bit-part holodeck character in *Voyager* is something of a come-down for the star of *Carry on England*. Though, on second thoughts . . .

9: Stephanie Beacham. As she was so good as Countess Regina Bartholomew, we'll let her off for doing *SeaQuest DSV* (as long as it doesn't happen again).

10: Marina Sirtis. We still love her, even if Deanna was a bit naff at times and she's a Spurs fan.
Whoops, looks like we forgot Patrick Stewart, that French accent being so convincing and all.

KEPTIN: Pavel Chekov's preferred form of address towards Captain Kirk, according to everyone who's ever written dialogue for him. Russians are more than welcome to join the American space programme in the enlightened world of the 23rd century, but at least we can still have a good old laugh at their silly accents.

KES: Title 'character' of Barry Hines's bestselling novel about a working-class boy and his beloved but ultimately doomed pet, a bird of prey. The book was originally called *A Kestrel for a Knave*, but this was shortened for the film version and for subsequent editions. Not to be confused in any way with Kes, *Voyager*'s way-cute space babe with appalling taste in blokes. Still, she finally grew out of that immature infatuation with Neelix (well what else would you call it? She'd been seeing him since she was about two years old!). It was a wise choice on her part: given the Talaxian's obvious fixation with under-age girls, he'd probably have dumped her by the time she was four anyway.

KIRK'S HORSE IMPRESSION: All right, we give up. How can we possibly write a spoof *Star Trek* book without mentioning William Shatner's hilarious spot of animal mimicry in 'Plato's Stepchildren'? The idea of it was that the telekinetic Parmen was torturing Kirk by making him run around on all fours with a dwarf on his back, giving out the occasional high-pitched whinny. It was seen to be a humiliating and degrading experience. So why was it acceptable for the script-writers to do exactly the same thing to Shatner? Just prior to this incident, Kirk and Spock had indulged in a bit of dancing at Parmen's behest. They got off lightly: many are the fans who would have taken this cast-iron opportunity to make the pair shag.

KLINGER, JAKE: Roger Lloyd-Pack's spoof Trekkie from the TV sitcom *2point4 Children*, as if some Trekkies can't spoof fandom all by themselves. 'Jake the Klingon' faked his own death for the sake of a scene in which the regular characters attended a funeral in *Star Trek* costumes (including a Tribble) and watched his coffin slide into the furnace to the strains of the original theme. To some of us, it provided a good laugh; to others, a good idea. Sadly, Jake proved to be unrealistically fickle and, for his second and third appearances, he had switched allegiances to *The Prisoner* and Gerry Anderson respectively. So what happened to the *Enterprise* mascot from the front of his van then, and can we have it?

KLINGON CULTURE: We can write whatever we like here as, if you've watched half as many *Next Gen* and *DS9* Klingon-based episodes as we have, your eyes will already have glazed over and you'll have passed on to the next entry.

KLINGONESE: Not content with having its main aliens spout gibberish whenever there isn't a universal translator about, *Star Trek* has adopted the comprehensive Klingon speech devised by linguist Marc Okrand (who must have plenty of time on his hands). The producers must be congratulated for their attention to detail (except for when they forgot to use it); some fans, however, must only be pointed at and mocked for their astonishingly sad reaction to this development. Yes, you all know what we mean – and if you've ever bought any of the dictionaries, language tapes, etc., or you know more than, say, no words of Klingon, you should hang your head in shame or, better still, just hang yourself you sad, irredeemable bastard. Anyway, now that we've insulted a good 50% of our readership, we should at least mention that conversational Klingon isn't half as hard to master as you might expect. This is simply because the number of phrases which might prove useful if approached by somebody who intends to begin an exchange in Klingonese can, in practice, be narrowed down to a rather conservative one: 'Sod off out of my face, you insane dribbling moron!' Even so, we can't risk the shame of actually looking at a Klingon dictionary for a translation of this, so a swift blow to the head must suffice for now.

KLINGONS: The ultimate *Star Trek* villains, which is why we don't think it made the greatest sense to have them change sides. Whatever their allegiance this week, there's nothing a certain section of fandom likes more than pretending to be these lump-headed warriors. It's all very well these people putting on the gear and talking in a funny Welsh-like language, but if they want to fully adopt the Klingon lifestyle they have to take it a step further – and we don't mean fitting low-wattage red light bulbs in their houses. For example, those of them able to hold down jobs ought to be prepared to assassinate their bosses if they are not performing up to scratch. And how many of them have actually died nobly in battle? Not a lot, we'd guess.

'KLINGONS ON THE STARBOARD BOW': Memorable lyrics from the classic pop anthem 'Star Trekkin'' by The Firm. A clever parody of the *Trek* universe, other insightful lines include: 'He's dead Jim, dead Jim, dead Jim, dead Jim. He's dead Jim, dead Jim, dead Jim, dead' and 'Boldly going forward, 'cos we can't find reverse.' Eat your heart out, Cole Porter. (See also 'HIGHLY ILLOGICAL'.)

KOROB: *TOS* alien who seemingly received fashion tips and hair-styling advice from Emperor Ming the Merciless. As it turned out, this appearance was merely a ruse to disguise his true form: a little blue furry puppet, complete with visible strings.

L

LAZARUS: Less-than-memorable first season *TOS* character. In fact we'd have forgotten about him entirely if it wasn't for that stupid-looking, wispy beard glued on to his face.*

* Oh, and his dumb spaceship (probably the crappiest one ever seen in a science fiction TV series or movie, and, yes, that does include Plan 9 From Outer Space*) which would have been better employed housing goldfish.*

'LEARNING CURVE': Nail-biting finale to *Voyager* season one, in which Tuvok attempts to assimilate some of the erstwhile Maquis members into the crew by having them jog around the corridors a few times; meanwhile, the ship is put at risk by some over-ripe cheese. Thrilling stuff.

LEETA THE DABO GIRL: Phwoar! Hubba, hubba, etc.

'LEGENDS NEVER DIE': Blurb on the cover of *The Return*. It's a *Star Trek* novel, so obviously we haven't read it, but apparently it's 'the astounding return of Captain Kirk as only William Shatner can tell it'. That's probably because only William Shatner can be bothered to tell it. Apparently, he first floated the idea as a possible eighth movie, just after filming Kirk's death scene in *Generations*. No doubt that would have been entirely for the fans' benefit, then. You can't blame him for hoping, though. After all, Kirk has always come back from the dead before – why should this time be any different? Come to think of it, Scotty still thought he was alive in 'Relics', didn't he? Perhaps they just hadn't had the funeral yet, as they were expecting their erstwhile captain to be improbably resurrected at any moment.

LENARA: Dax's lesbian lover . . . well almost, which is a pity. Her Artificial Wormhole project was a bit of a feeble excuse for going to *Deep Space Nine* – after all, there's a perfectly good real one there already.

LESTER, JANICE: Yet another of Kirk's conquests – but then you already knew that because she was in *The Original Series* and she has a girl's name, right? More significantly, Janice achieved her lifelong ambition of becoming a ship's captain in 'Turnabout Intruder'. But, just a sec, didn't we say she was in *TOS* (albeit the very last episode of it)? Blimey, a female captain – a bit radical for American television in the '60s, don't you think? Oh no, hold on a minute . . . seems she had to take over Kirk's body first. So everyone obeyed her, but only because she had a penis at the time. Phew, that's OK then.

LIBERIA: Country in, erm . . . somewhere that has featured *Star Trek* on its coinage. We can't understand why all true Trekkies don't up and move to this *Trek*-friendly nation right away; unless they're put off by the seemingly unfavourable exchange rate – it costs five quid just for one $1 coin.

LIFE-SUPPORT BELTS: Fantastic innovations from *The Animated Series*, which allowed the crew to gallivant about in airless environments without spacesuits, fully protected by a Ready Brek-type glow. They even doubled as nifty force fields and prevented Scotty from being crushed by a big bit of machinery. Sheer brilliance!

LIGHTS: Extremely low-budget aliens formerly from Zetar.

LONDON KINGS: Unlikely 21st-century baseball team mentioned in *TNG*'s 'The Big Goodbye'. The only way baseball could ever become popular in the UK capital is if fans of football teams like Arsenal, Chelsea, Spurs, etc. got too fed up of seeing their teams beaten by Manchester United. *DS9*, on the other hand, made a reference to a team that sounded perfectly feasible in the *Trek* Universe: the Pike City Pioneers. (See also BASEBALL – if you can be bothered.)

LOVE BOAT, THE: Saccharin American TV series, with which we are thankfully no longer inflicted. Some fans said that the constant sexual tension between Picard and Crusher on the one hand, and Riker and Troi on the other, made early episodes of *The Next Generation* seem like *The Love Boat in Space* (see 'GET A LIFE!'). Perhaps inspired by such criticism, Patrick Stewart spoofed his own *Next Gen* character in *Saturday Night Live*'s *The Love Boat: The Next Generation* sketch, and it would have worked too, if only they'd thought to include some jokes in the script.

LUVVIES: A regular column in *Private Eye*, 'devoted to gems from the acting profession'. For some reason, its compilers saw fit to quote a *Daily Telegraph* interview with William Shatner. 'He is a classical humanist,' Shatner says of Captain Kirk. 'I do admire the classical Greek philosophy of balance and unity, in their drama, in their statuary. It was the greatest flowering of mankind . . .' He goes on to list Alexander the Great's qualifications for helming the *Enterprise*, before pointing out that '*Star Trek* is a spiritual journey . . . That's why it has proved so popular, so enduring. It is a journey where no psyche has gone before.' All this is nothing new, of course. Shatner has always stood up for *Star Trek* . . . well, for *The Original Series* anyway. Far be it from us to mention his appeals to fans to boycott *The Next Generation* on the grounds that Kirk was a more three-dimensional character than Picard.* Funny, really – we could have sworn that Gene Roddenberry said he was just Captain Hornblower in space. Mind you, he said that about Picard too.

* *In one obvious way, he was right.*

LYNCH, LELAND T: Chief engineering officer on the *Enterprise* at the time that Tasha Yar was brutally slain by a tar pit. Despite being a minor character, he displayed the typical Starfleet compulsion of forever having to reveal that his middle initial was T. Perhaps, in the 24th century, the legend of James T Kirk has assured that this has become some sort of a status symbol. (See T.)

M

MADDOX, BRUCE: Starfleet scientist who wanted to take Data apart to find out how he worked. Data objected to this and a court hearing ensued to clarify the android's legal status. The thing about *Star Trek* courtroom dramas – apart from them all being short enough to make legal history – is that the outcome is never in doubt: we all know that the defendant, in this case Data, is still going to be around for the next episode. But this particular trial was even more lacking in tension than usual – the result was a certainty as soon as Riker was named as prosecutor.

MAKING OF STAR TREK, THE: The first ever *Star Trek* reference work, originally published even before the series was cancelled – which shows just how early it was. Since then it has been reprinted practically an infinite number of times, and no doubt revised and expanded too – it certainly needed to be.

TEN AMUSING THINGS REVEALED IN *THE MAKING OF STAR TREK*

1: The series might have been set in the far-flung future of 1995.
2: Another suggested date was 2995. Well, technology wouldn't change much in a thousand years, would it?
3: Early sketches of the *Enterprise* made it look like some washing-up liquid bottles stuck to a football.

4: 'Do they use flush toilets?' was one of the more intriguing questions posed by the book about life in the future. Sadly, the answer was not forthcoming. Do they use toilets at all?

5: The mighty Starfleet was to have had a grand total of twelve starships.

6: The *Enterprise* was to have been armed with lasser beams. Jean-Luc Picard wouldn't have been impressed: even spelt properly, these weapons wouldn't dent the communications shields of the *Enterprise D*.

7: The highly versatile tricorder apparently came into being following the suggestion that, to give her more (i.e. something) to do, the captain's yeoman ought to carry some equipment. 'And she's got some pretty good equipment already,' quipped Gene Roddenberry.

8: Long before 'The Chase' attempted to explain that huge coincidence of humanoids being everywhere in the galaxy, 'The Similar Worlds Concept' was responsible for the proliferation. In all fairness, the intention was not to have every planet populated by men in silver jumpsuits: 'to give continual variety, use will of course be made of wigs, skin colouration, changes in noses, hands, ears and even the occasional addition of tails and such.' Latterday *Star Trek* producers: please note the absence of lumpy foreheads from that list.

9: Not only did the volume provide a fascinating insight into the programme's origins, it gave a tantalising preview of the future: '*Star Trek*'s third season will emphasise the Vulcan philosophy of universal brotherhood via an unusually shaped medallion Mr Spock will receive from home and begin to wear.' Hmm, must have got lost in the post.

10: James Kirk is sensitive.

MALTZ: Klingon officer portrayed by John Larroquette in *Star Trek III – The Search for Spock*. Apparently mindful of the great big sticky Mars bar on his forehead, he nicknamed his character 'Chocolate Maltz'. (See also QUCH.)

MAN FROM UNCLE, THE: '60s spy series notable for giving to the world the first TV pairing of William Shatner and Leonard Nimoy. Sadly missing from this early collaboration, though, was the fervent sexual chemistry that many fans bizarrely perceive as being fundamental to their later on-screen relationship.

McCOY'S MAGIC BLUE SHIRT: It's absolutely amazing the way it can transform itself from the ordinary long-sleeved version to the shiny short-sleeved medical one and back again before you can say 'continuity error'.

McGIVERS, MARLA: Mini-skirted historian chosen by Kirk to join a landing party, not because he could remember her name or anything, but because he'd seen her around. Imagine his surprise, then, when she went all ga-ga over Khan and ignored the captain altogether. He later bollocked her (though not in the way he'd hoped) for allowing romantic feelings to affect her performance. A distant pot-like voice can be heard to utter racist, anti-kettle remarks.

MÈRDE: Expletive uttered several times by that consummate Frenchman Jean-Luc Picard. It is actually French for 'shit', and was thus no doubt the production team's attempt to look hard and grown-up by sneaking swear words past the censors. Just in case you didn't know.

METHOD ACTING: Perhaps the way to get an ongoing role in a *Star Trek* series. Michael Dorn claims to have bagged the part of the Klingon Worf by going through the audition process in character. He didn't do much, though: he just ignored the other actors in the waiting-room and made a point of not smiling at the panel. You could easily have trumped him by, say, turning up with an Airfix model of Sydney Opera House – painted brown – on your head, talking in Klingonese, attacking the panel with a bat'leth, and

119

claiming that rejection would be a serious insult against your honour which would force you to challenge Rick Berman to a duel. This approach obviously wouldn't work in every situation though, else one could conclude that the part of the insatiable Lwaxana Troi went to whoever was sleeping with Gene Roddenberry at the time – which would be a ludicrous accusation.

METRONS: Race of camp aliens who enjoy watching rough, sweaty men wrestle.

MISTER COMPUTER: How Moriarty addressed the *Enterprise*'s computer, despite having heard its unmistakably female intonations. Thought this bloke was supposed to be dead clever. Still, it could have been worse, he could have called it Mrs Roddenberry.

MONA LISA: Leonardo da Vinci's beautiful portrait of an enigmatic lady is perhaps the most famous and best-loved work of art the world over. But this didn't stop SkyBox from desecrating it in the cause of flogging their 1994 series of *Star Trek* trading cards. 'With a Stroke of the Brush, a Generation Gap is Crossed,' they boasted, above a reproduction of the painting to which the Starship *Enterprise* had been added (over Mona's right shoulder). SkyBox's implication was that their cards were worthy of a place in the Louvre alongside da Vinci's masterpiece. Not so, although a full set of 100 of these over-priced, foil-stamped pics plus all the rare triptych panels would probably cost about the same (we have no idea what a triptych panel is, but it sounds crap). In the event, they fitted nicely onto the walls of comic book shops alongside SkyBox's other *Star Trek* series and hundreds of similar attempts to extort cash from gullible completists.

MONK: The role that James Tiberius Kirk would take on in *Star Trek V*, according to persistent rumours before the film's release. Yeah, sure. Of course, holy orders may have so evolved by the time of the 23rd century that the abstinence rule has been replaced by, say, one about shagging an awful lot.

MOONS: Hmmm, we seem to have a problem here. It was clearly established in *The Original Series* that Vulcan had none of these orbiting satellites, and yet, in *The Animated Series*, there they are as bright as ... erm, night. So which version takes precedence? We need only look to the movies to provide their casting vote ... and *The Animated Series* it is. (See also T.)

MOREAU, MARLENA: Sultry siren who became Kirk's sex slave in the mirror universe. Upon his return, he met her counterpart for the first time – or so we were led to believe in 'Mirror, Mirror'. But since then, the time-lines have changed so that he encountered 'Lieutenant' Benjamin Sisko instead, as recounted at the end of 'Trials and Tribble-ations'. Sisko must have been pretty keen to talk to Kirk: contrary to what he later told the Department of Temporal Investigations, he must have taken the *Defiant* back in time again to a few weeks before the Tribble incident in his pursuit of an appropriate moment to approach him. However, the fact that Kirk paid any attention at all to Sisko – a male officer, as opposed to the short-skirted piece of totty who would otherwise have brought him his reports – is pretty unrealistic, and his lustful expression during the short conversation seems not entirely appropriate. It may be a minor violation, given that Sisko had just prevented a radical rewriting of history – but Kirk would surely never forgive his successor were he to learn that he had deprived him of an almost definite conquest.

MORIARTY: The original arch-nemesis in fiction, Moriarty could match Sherlock Holmes deduction for deduction, but his goals were diametrically opposed to the master detective's own. Many writers have since followed Arthur Conan Doyle's splendid example and furnished their heroes with highly successful villainous opposites: the good renegade Time Lord, Doctor Who, has the bad renegade Time Lord, the Master; the grim do-gooder, Batman, has the clownish psychopath, the Joker; and Dennis the Menace has Walter the Softy. Somehow, though, the writers of *Star Trek* managed to misunderstand the concept, so their version of Moriarty was

... erm, Moriarty. It took the holodeck, as usual, to bring life to this (uniquely sentient) creation. But the dastardly fiend caused almost as many problems for the series' producers as he did for Picard and co. Mistakenly assuming that he was in the public domain, they ended up with all manner of copyright problems. Quite right, too: they wouldn't like it if the Klingons turned up in *Friends* or something, would they?

<hr>

TEN CURIOUS SHERLOCK HOLMES-BASED *STAR TREK* FACTS

1: Daniel Davis played Moriarty in *TNG,* which we could have mentioned above, but we're really going to struggle to get ten of these.

2: Inspector Lestrade was portrayed in *TNG* by Alan Shearman . . . hey, we're coming to the good ones.

3: *Undiscovered Country* director and co-script-writer Nicholas Meyer is a big fan of Holmes, and the author of two pastiche novels featuring the great detective. So it was no big surprise when, in that film, Spock alludes to Holmes being one of his ancestors. Presumably, this is on his mother's side.

4: The film version of Meyer's novel *The Seven Percent Solution* is notable for featuring, in Nicol Williamson and Robert Duval, the oddest, most miscast Holmes and Watson ever. Well, at least until Data and Geordi had a go in 'Elementary, Dear Data'.

5: Leonard Nimoy, a logical choice (ho ho), played Holmes in the educational short 'The Hidden Motive', and toured in William Gillette's imaginatively titled play *Sherlock Holmes*.

6: William Shatner was really rather good as Stapleton in a '70s TV movie version of *The Hound of the Baskervilles* that was really rather shit (dog shit, even).

7: Actors John Neville and Christopher Plummer have both appeared in *Star Trek*, and they've both played Holmes in films in which the Baker Street sleuth takes on Jack the Ripper. Though obviously neither did enough to prevent the notorious killer from turning up again in the 23rd century for 'Wolf in the Fold'.

8: 'Elementary, Dear Data' is a play on 'Elementary, my dear Watson', an oft-quoted phrase which Holmes never actually uttered in Doyle's canon. Hmm, just like Captain Kirk has been associated with a famous phrase he never used (see 'BEAM ME UP, SCOTTY').

9: The follow up to 'Elementary, Dear Data' was 'Ship in a Bottle'. We don't remember Holmes saying that either ... OK, you come up with some better ones then.

10: Oh sod it.

MORN: The name given, belatedly, to Mark Allen Shepherd's semi-regular 'alien barfly' character in *Deep Space Nine*. His demeanour as he sat at Quark's Bar reminded the production team so much of the popular character Norm Peterson from *Cheers* that they christened him accordingly. Although they haven't admitted it yet, the same logic must have applied when Jonathan Frakes's *Next Generation* commander was named with a partial anagram of 'Kirk'. But if that's the case, why isn't Tuvok called Mr Blackspock or something, and why didn't Beverly Crusher just name her son Tawt?*

* *Actually, by a strange coincidence, the actor who plays* Voyager's *holographic doctor is called Robert Picardo. He couldn't have chosen the surname just because he's bald, now could he? Naw, surely not.***
** *But, spookily, Jean-Luc's brother – introduced in 'Family' and killed off in 'All Good Things' – was actually called Robert Picard. And he was bald, too.*

'MOST WILL BE MUCH MORE INTERESTING': Jean-Luc Picard's prediction for the *Enterprise*'s future missions, as given at the end of the pilot episode, 'Encounter at Farpoint'. Well, he said it.

MOTIONLESS PICTURE, THE: Mildly amusing but highly accurate nickname given to the first *Star Trek* movie by just about everyone that's seen it.

M'RESS: Gorgeous feline alien *Enterprise* bridge-crew member in *The Animated Series*. She was yet another sound reason for including the cartoon adventures in the official *Star Trek* canon. Had that been the case, M'Ress could have been included in the subsequent movies and personified by, as a for instance, Michelle Pfeiffer.

MUDD'S ANGELS: *TOS* noveliser James Blish evidently believed the two episodes starring the entrepreneurial Harry Mudd to be a cut above the others, and so gave them a book of their own and added a self-penned Mudd story in the process. We don't know what it was about – but, going from the book's title, we assume the eponymous rogue formed a detective agency staffed by bimbos.

TEN SUGGESTED STORY TITLES, SHOULD HARRY MUDD EVER CONSIDER A CAREER MOVE

1: Mudd Pie. He runs a bakery.
2: Mudd Flats. He enters the accommodation to let business.
3: Mudd Slide. A children's playground seems like a promising venture.
4: Mudd Guard. Next up, a Group Four-style security firm.
5: Mudd Wrestling. Back to exploiting women.
6: Muddy Boots. As a last resort, he becomes a shoe salesman.
7: Muddy Waters. He, erm, finds fame as a blues musician.
8: Mudd in your eye. Someone's already done this as a book title; we haven't read it, of course, but we expect he starts up as an optician.

9: Muddjahadin. He forms a force of fundamentalist freedom fighters (if you'll pardon the alliteration) dedicated to the expulsion of foreign invaders.

10: Oh dear, we can't think of any more. Suppose you could say we're in a bit of a muddle . . . Oh well, that's close enough.

MULTIPLE TECHNIQUES: What Data was programmed with, sexually, or at least that's what he told Tasha Yar. But come on, really, why would Dr Soong have bothered with such details? This surely betrays the intended function of his android as not the walking encyclopedia-cum-computer that he has become, but rather as an artificially intelligent dildo for those long nights in space.

MUSTARD-COLOURED SHIRTS (AKA GOLD SHIRTS): In the days of *TOS* these denoted a command post, while red shirts were worn by those in security positions. Nowadays this colour system has been reversed – a bold and fair-minded step by Starfleet's hierarchy. (See SHIRTS, RED if you don't appreciate why.)

***MYSTERY SCIENCE THEATER* (sic) *3000*:** American TV series which lampooned various crappy B movies by re-screening them but having a trio of animated characters pass comment throughout. *Star Trek V – The Final Frontier* was precisely the type of film they had set their sights on, but Paramount didn't really get the joke, so they did it for fun only and never dared to broadcast the results. Still, copies have made their way into the hands of collectors, even in this country, so fans can now enjoy *Star Trek V** the *MST3K* way. The main observations, though – that there are lots of rocks and that the scripted puns aren't funny – are less than incisive. Watch the original movie with a couple of mates and a few cans of beer and you'll probably get the same effect.

* *Yes, we said 'enjoy Star Trek V' – weird, isn't it?*

125

N

NAKED: State of undress in which, according to the dictates of their culture, Ferengi women must be at all times. So must any females who visit their homeworld, so it's no wonder they chose to kidnap the Trois. A very few Ferengi women have broken with convention and disgracefully go around wearing clothes; it is, of course, these fully dressed women who tend to turn up on *Deep Space Nine*. What is apparent from this is that the programme's makers are fearful of upsetting the prudish powers-that-be, with their out-moded regulations. If *DS9* is ever to be regarded as truly ground-breaking, it needs to go one better than *TNG* – which boldly showed Picard's butt – and do an all-nude episode. We suggest that Dax and Kira go on a diplomatic mission to Ferenginar – perhaps taking Leeta the Dabo girl – and, respectful of its cultural traditions . . .

'NAKED NOW, THE': Early *TNG* episode which, sadly, didn't live up to its name. In order to combat a virus with symptoms manifesting themselves as intoxication, the *Enterprise D* crew accessed the files of the original vessel, as the same virus had swept through a similar plot in *TOS*'s 'The Naked Time' (which didn't live up to its name either). Fortunately, they didn't think to use the same trick again in 'Unnatural Selection', as the ageing disease encountered therein was a completely different one to that contracted in 'The Deadly Years', albeit with identical and, it has to be said, unusual symptoms.

NDEFO, OBI: Surprisingly, this isn't a bizarre alien from some distant galaxy, it's the name of a guest actor in *Deep Space Nine*.

NEMESIS: Working title for the ninth *Star Trek* movie – replacing *Millennium*, as that was bound to confuse people into thinking it was a crossover with, erm, *Millennium*. The movie – which will probably have another name by the time this sees print – is being brought forward a year to avoid clashing with the fourth (or first, or whatever) *Star Wars* movie. Well, Paramount, that might make financial sense, but don't you realise that with this act of capitulation you'll be providing ammo for the *Star Wars* v *Star Trek* net-nerds? According to the earliest reports, Picard is to be promoted to admiral – dunno why, but that seems a little familiar somehow. And Riker will be made a captain. Fair enough, as long as he's prepared to shave his head.

NEPOTISM, TOTAL LACK OF: It is well known that, when Gene Roddenberry first envisaged his 23rd-century epic, he wanted a woman as the first officer of the Starship *Enterprise* – and, after an extensive search, it was decided that one M Leigh Hudec (by coincidence, Roddenberry's real-life partner) was ideally suited to take on the role of Number One in the pilot episode. Unfortunately, studio executives failed to share this particular vision, and so the character was ungraciously dropped. All was not lost though, as this left Majel free to more than adequately fill Nurse Chapel's blue mini-dress. She applied for this role as Majel Barrett, clearly determined to win it on merit alone and not on the strength of her name. Her gamble paid off. Majel, of course, is also a gifted voice artist – and so it was only natural that her talents should come to the fore when *Star Trek* became an animated series. She portrayed the cat-like alien M'Ress. And Randi Bryce. And Lora. And Theela. But she was cruelly robbed of the chance to play Lieutenant Uhura when, for some reason, the studio cast Nichelle Nichols in that part instead. Not to worry: when *Star Trek* returned to live-action and moved onto the big screen, Majel was back again to celebrate the long-overdue and well-deserved advancement of Christine Chapel to doctor. In the meantime, the hunt was on for an actress capable of voicing all of Starfleet's computers in *The Next Generation* (and, ultimately, its successors). Out of thousands of candidates, Majel Barrett Roddenberry came instantly to the fore, no doubt due to her adept handling of the voice of Gary Seven's computer, Beta 5, in the *TOS* episode/series pilot, 'Assignment: Earth'. By now, Majel was a little older and a lot more experienced, which gave her the confidence to attempt the challenging character part of Lwaxana Troi, also for *Next Gen*. As luck would have it, she was considered the best person for the role – and so successfully did she meet this challenge that Lwaxana also crossed over into *Deep Space Nine*. Her long and distinguished association with the *Star Trek* legend continues.

NOG, CAPTAIN: In one of those possible futures that keep cropping up in *Star Trek*, Nog attained command of the *Defiant*: an achievement that hopefully compensated for the fact that he obviously stopped growing at an early age.

NOMAD: Not-too-distant cousin of V'Ger – though if the makers of the first *Star Trek* film had to plunder an original TV episode to find a plot, you'd have expected them to pick one of the better ones. On second thoughts 'The Changeling' probably is one of the better ones. Nomad is a typical *Star Trek* villain, i.e., a self-important, habitual killer of people in red shirts – it even kills Mr Scott. But let's face it, Scotty was asking for it going around dressed like that. Fortunately, following a word in its antennae from Kirk, Nomad realised it wasn't the done thing to kill series regulars and resurrected the unfortunate chief engineer – as you do.

TEN REGULAR CHARACTERS WHO HAVE DIED, INCLUDING ONE WHO HAS ACTUALLY STAYED DEAD SO FAR

1: Chekov.
2: Kim.

'NON SEQUITUR': Ensign Kim wakes up at the beginning of this episode to find himself on Earth. It seems as if all his exploits aboard *Voyager* have been a dream (if only), and he is back at home with a successful career and a cracking girlfriend. And yet he's determined to get back to the middle of nowhere with his *Voyager* buddies. Perhaps he enjoys being killed on a regular basis?

NORMAN: Head android on a world that Chekov thought was even better than Leningrad (an understandable lack of foresight from the script-writers there, but worth a mention all the same). Not surprisingly, Norman turned out to be less matey than first thought, but fortunately he fell for the old 'everything I say is a lie and I'm lying now' trick. Gets 'em every time.

NOSE: Odo must be a bit of a poor shape-changer really, as he still can't master this simple feature of the human face* despite the fact that all the other Founders can and are busy gadding about in other people's likenesses (Bashir's being a particular favourite). It makes you wonder what else Odo hasn't got right yet – though, no doubt, if he ever cops off with Kira, he'll turn out to be 'fully functional in that department'.** After all, since when were any two *Star Trek* races unable to mate?

* *He can do a dog's nose all right.*
** *If not, he could always do the German Shepherd again, as he's bound to have the dog's bollocks.*

NOVELS, POCKET BOOK: We did intend to include full in-depth coverage of these important corner-stones of the universe of *Star Trek* merchandising – but there are bloody hundreds of the things, so we didn't. (We didn't read any either.)

OATFIELD *STAR TREK: THE NEXT GENERATION* SHERBERT-FILLED FRUIT-FLAVOUR DROPS: Not only do they have a logo and a picture of the *Enterprise* on the wrapping; not only is one of sixteen holographic stickers secreted within (but for 'holographic' read 'silver'); not only can you send off for a *Next Gen* poster for a quid; but they taste dead good too. What more can you ask?

OATH OF CELIBACY: Obviously aware of his reputation, Lt. Ilia made a point of mentioning her vow to Captain Kirk (by this time, a porker in more than one sense of the word) as soon as she met him. A mistake, surely: he'd only regard something like that as a challenge.

OCAMPA: Kes's race. As you'd expect of a species from the other side of the galaxy, they are very different from most of those encountered in *Star Trek* in that they don't have lumpy foreheads; of course they do have funny-shaped pointed ears (this is *Star Trek* after all). But, uniquely, they possess incredible mental powers enabling the psychokinetic manipulation of matter. The upshot of this is that they can grow nice flowers and brew tea.

OCETT, GUL: The first female Cardassian to have appeared in *Star Trek*. The honour of playing her went to former *Avengers* girl Linda Thorson – though we'd better not say too much more. We don't want to risk getting the book pulped or anything (an in-joke that the authors of *The New Trek Programme Guide* won't find at all amusing).

TEN *TREK* GUEST STARS WHO'VE BEEN IN OTHER TELEFANTASY SHOWS AS WELL AS *STAR TREK*

1: Lee Meriwether was a regular on *The Time Tunnel*, a series in which the temporally misplaced protagonists did sensible things like attempting to prevent the Titanic from sinking!

2: Michael Ansara (Klingon Kang) appeared as a villain in the first season of *Buck Rogers in the 25th Century* (which was a bit crap really).

3: Barbara Luna was married to budgie man Hawk in the second season of *Buck Rogers in the 25th Century* (radically different from the first season, but still crap). She was lucky enough to be killed off in the first story.

4: John Hoyt (Dr Philip Boyce in the pilot) lost out to DeForest Kelley when it came to playing the ship's doctor, but a part in *Voyage to the Bottom of the Sea* might have been some consolation.

5: *The Addams Family*'s Lurch, Ted Cassidy, was in *The Original Series* (and the movie Lurch was in *Next Gen*, but that doesn't count in this list).

6: *Batman*'s the Riddler, Frank Gorshin, interestingly enough played a *Star Trek* character more reminiscent of Two Face (well, we thought it was interesting).

7: Nick Tate. Apart from the theme tunes, the only good thing about *Space: 1999* was Aussie pilot Alan Carter.

8: John Collicos was in *Battlestar Galactica* and that's all we're going to say about that particular series.

9: Stanley Adams, who excelled as Cyranno Jones in the Tribbles episodes, once had a part in *Lost In Space*.

10: Try as we might, we can't seem to forget *SeaQuest DSV*'s Stephanie Beacham.

OFFICIAL BEEPY BADGE: What Home Entertainment offered for sale to eager fans, though it looked more like a Starfleet communicator to us. More evidence that the company isn't as clued up as it might be can be found on its specially issued set of *Star Trek* stamps, the rather nondescript titles for which include: 'Spock's Father' (Sarek) and 'Futuristic City' (the citadel on Rigel VII). Best of all, the classic and much-seen photograph of Captain Kirk covered in Tribbles is described as 'Kirk with Animal'. Well, we thought it was funny.

OFFICIAL *STAR TREK* CASSETTE PLAYER: An absolutely crucial item of merchandise for the collection of any true Trekkie, this one. Just imagine the alternative: having to play all those *Star Trek* audio books on just any old common or garden cassette player. It doesn't bear thinking about.

OFFICIAL STAR TREK FACT FILES, THE: This sort of thing was quite in vogue once: the weekly collection of looseleaf pages which eventually built into a complete encyclopedia. But then readers realised that few of them ever got past the third issue, and they died out. This one has a better chance than some of making it, we suppose (if it's been cancelled already, please remember we wrote this months ago!), though once the splendour of the free binder with issue one has worn off, some readers might think to calculate that a full run of 104 issues will cost £202.80, barring unforeseen price increases. Even the SkyBox customisable card game sounds almost worth buying in comparison. Oh yes, and by the time they're all out, they'll be well out of date, won't they? Hence the inevitable (if sales are good enough first time round) run of supplement/replacement sheets. But, oh, we'd fork out the whole cost happily if only they'd deigned to cover *TAS*!

OKONA: His name was pronounced O'Conner, presumably to give him the air of a lovable Irish rogue (like O'Brien, but not much). He almost caused an interplanetary incident when accused of getting some high-up's daughter in the club; though going by the speed in which he shagged his way through the female contingent of the *Enterprise D*'s crew, it's not surprising he was the prime suspect. Okona wasn't really a man of his time: had he been born a century earlier they'd probably have given him a Federation Starship to command.

OLD MAN: Sisko's nickname for Dax. Bloody hell, is he blind, or just confused because she's got a bloke's name?

ONE, NUMBER: The full name assigned to Majel Barrett's character in 'The Cage' (and 'The Menagerie'). Gender nonspecific it may be, but NBC weren't fooled: they weren't having any girlies in command positions and that was the end of it. Had this original version of the *Star Trek* pilot been accepted, however, we are forced to conclude that Number One would have had to take a proper name at some point in the ensuing series. Or perhaps she really was supposed to be so shallow. The legacy of all this lives on today: Number One, like the rest of her crew, is prime material to be used in fan fiction, spin-off novels and comic books. The only trouble is, the writers have to turn cartwheels to avoid referring to her by anything other than her rank, as this would constitute – heaven forbid – an addition to Gene Roddenberry's perfect work.* Good job she was never promoted really: that would only have caused needless confusion.

* *Though one of the* Best of Trek *books dared to claim that she was Christine Chapel's sister.*

1,701: The number of Picard and Tasha Yar action figures that Playmates produced in a special limited edition. What's more, they expected collectors to be pleased about this. In an ideal world they might have been: here, in this hypothetical parallel universe, only 1,701 people would have wanted them and dealers wouldn't have put such exorbitant mark-ups on the things. Stung by criticism of their tactics, Playmates decided to bump up the production run of the last figure in the series, Lt. Barclay, to a staggering 3,000. 'Kinnel!

TEN JEAN-LUC PICARD FIGURES THAT WEREN'T LIMITED TO A RUN OF 1,701 (BUT NOT INCLUDING THOSE WITH HIM IN VARIATIONS OF HIS REGULAR CAPTAIN'S UNIFORM . . . AND THERE ARE A FEW OF THOSE)

1: Young Picard as Starfleet Academy cadet.
2: As a Romulan from 'Unification'.
3: Wearing a *Deep Space Nine* uniform.
4: As Galen from 'Gambit'.
5: As Locutus of Borg from 'The Best of Both Worlds' (black).
6: As Locutus of Borg from 'The Best of Both Worlds' (silver).
7: As Dixon Hill, for thrilling holodeck adventures.
8: In *Generations* uniform as he wasn't seen in *Generations*.
9: In spacesuit from *First Contact*.
10: Old Picard from 'All Good Things'.

ORDERS: Despite the militaristic structure of Starfleet, they're a bit lax about these things really, else why would so many people get on in the organisation despite a seemingly complete inability to obey them? It's all very well doing what you're told when it's yer old mate Jim or Benjamin in the command chair – but along comes someone like Captain Jellico or Commodore Decker and suddenly it's 'We don't like strangers in these here parts', and you've got mutiny on your hands. Sometimes we wonder why Starfleet even bother. If you were an admiral and you had to send an urgent subspace communication along the lines of 'Please don't go off and fight the Borg' or 'Don't you dare rescue Captain Kirk from that Klingon prison', you'd just find something better to waste your time on, wouldn't you?

OVER THE HILL: The last couple of movies to feature the original crew showed just how wide of the mark the make-up people were when they visualised Kirk, Scotty and the rest suffering from an advanced ageing disease in 'The Deadly Years'. If only they'd thought to use some sort of padding* on the actors instead of sprinkling talcum powder over their hair, the results might have been a bit more convincing.

That episode's competency hearing to establish whether Kirk was too senile to command the ship (he was) – in which various crew members described incidents of the captain's memory lapses that we'd already seen minutes earlier – was blatant padding, but of the wrong type.

OXO CUBE: Oh dear, oh dear. After being admired for over two decades for its innovative ship designs, *Star Trek* spoilt it all by introducing the fearsome Borg and having their vessels resemble nothing more than one of these popular stock cubes. Starfleet have tried all they can think of in the continuing battle to repulse the cybernetic horrors – but all they really have to do is to shoot some boiling water at them or, if feeling more ambitious, build a giant, remote-controlled pair of fingers and get them to crumble the attacking fleet to powder.

P

PANCAKES, FLYING: The nearest description of the parasitic creatures that got Spock's back up in 'Operation Annihilate'.

PARALLEL UNIVERSES: Ever-popular story-line basis which allows the regulars to play themselves with evil overtones and better costumes. The producers of *DS9* ought to have realised that their first mirror universe crossover could prove successful enough to warrant a sequel,* and refrained from killing off too many counterparts. That way they wouldn't have had to bump up Rom's part (if you'll pardon the expression) or bring in characters from other series to fill the gaps. Tuvok's involvement might have buggered up any possibility of a mirror universe-set *Voyager* escapade too, if they hadn't done that already by writing out the Federation there. Though that probably wouldn't stop them – considering the massive coincidence of all the regular *DS9* characters turning up in close proximity to the mirror version of Terrok Nor, what's the betting that Janeway, Paris and the rest haven't all accidentally stumbled into the mirror delta quadrant?

* *That fine* Original Series *episode 'Mirror, Mirror' got a sequel too, but it was in a comic. Even so, it was almost tempting enough to read.*

PAR'MACH: Klingonese for 'love', but the word has 'more aggressive overtones'. Well it would have, wouldn't it? As demonstrated by both Dax and Quark, Klingon lovemaking is a bit of a bumpy ride, necessitating a visit to sickbay for any unfortunate non-Klingon who happens to have been involved. This has surely got to take some of the fun out of it, not to mention the embarrassment of having your local doctor know all there is to know about your sex life. Bashir, for example, is well acquainted with the ins and outs (so to speak) of Worf and Dax's relationship. Not recommended.

'PAST PROLOGUE': A short story on which Jake Sisko was working at the time of Nog's return to *Deep Space Nine*. He claimed it was fiction, but presumably it was a factual account of the incident in which Major Kira helped out a former colleague in the Bajoran Underground, shortly after Jake's arrival on the station.

PEN: Not-so-futuristic writing implement used by Jake Sisko in *DS9*'s answer to 'All Good Things'. No wonder he only managed to get two books out in twenty years or whatever.

PENIS: The missing word from the second line of Data's limerick in 'The Naked Now'. So now you know.

PHYSICIST: Sulu's job in the second *Star Trek* pilot. Yet, by the time the series proper came along, he was a humble helmsman. Surely a demotion not befitting Roddenberry's view of etc., etc.

PICARD MANOEUVRE, THE: Some spaceship-type thingy that was pioneered by Captain Jean-Luc Picard, but if you really want to know about it then check out one of those many publications which cares about that sort of techno-babble stuff. The label has also been applied by fans and professionals alike to Patrick Stewart's habit of tugging at his uniform tunic whenever it rides up, although why he doesn't get one that fits is beyond us.

PIGS IN SPACE: Gene Roddenberry might have decreed that *The Animated Series* was not canonical (bastard), but at least he made no such pronouncements about this porcine Muppet version. The exploits of Captain Link Hogthrob,

Doctor Strangepork and Miss Piggy could very well have happened in, say, the delta quadrant of the *Star Trek* universe. Indeed, the *Muppets Tonight* sequel – *Swine Trek: The Next Generation* – managed a fantastic crossover episode, with Leonard Nimoy appearing as . . . well, as himself, sadly. But then, we all know that he is Mr Spock anyway (see *I AM NOT SPOCK*).

PIKE, CHRISTOPHER: Former *Enterprise* captain who was badly mutilated when an accident in the line of duty forced him to be played by a different actor. His predicament showed up the level of medical cover provided by a parsimonious Starfleet. After all, even in the 20th century, *Next Gen* star Professor Stephen Hawking had a proper voice synthesizer. So, 300 years on and with technology having improved by leaps and bounds, what did they give Pike to communicate with? A flashing light, that's what. Pretty unfair, we think. Incidentally, Kirk's predecessor once considered resigning his Starfleet commission and taking up slave trading. Well, he'd have been really popular on the *Enterprise D*.

PINK KARATE TOPS: Gym apparel worn, over what look suspiciously like tights, in 'Charlie X'. After this, it was impossible to regard Captain Kirk in quite the same light again.

PINOCCHIO: Carlo Collodi's fictional puppet boy, to whom Lieutenant Commander Data is consistently compared, much to our irritation (even Riker was at it in 'The Measure of a Man', when he made a better job of prosecuting his old friend than anybody else in the universe would in that situation). Since when did Pinocchio have an evil twin? And in which episode was it established that Data's nose grows when he tells lies, or that he is made of wood (it would have meant a few splinters for Tasha Yar if he was)? No, the only similarity we can see between the two characters is that both wanted to be human – and in different ways at that, as Pinocchio clearly had human feelings from the start. So what, anyway? When was there ever an artificial life form in fiction which didn't share this desire? In fact, the story of Data's emotional awakening is much more reminiscent of that of the Vision, the 'synthezoid' member of Marvel's *Avengers* – and no one ever accused his creators of plagiarising Collodi, did they? Well OK then, perhaps they did.

PIZZA: Acne-inducing foodstuff that had to be scoffed in great amounts when Pizza Hut offered a range of cheap plastic *Star Trek* models to their customers. The models came in kit form, although happily they only had four or five slot-together components, so you didn't have to bugger about for hours with fiddly bits of plastic and glue. Once you'd eaten your way through enough deep crusts to get three or four *Enterprise*s, you even stood a fair chance of getting one with all the right parts in the correct quantities.

'PLANET HELL': Multi-layered planet set used in many, many episodes of *Star Trek* from *TNG* onwards, as an alternative to location filming. Impressive though it is, there's a limit to the number of angles it can be shot from and the number of lighting effects that can be utilised upon it, which is why so many *Star Trek* worlds look suspiciously similar. Still, it's an improvement on the days when they just scattered a few polystyrene rocks about the place (see ROCKS). Presumably, it was by way of an in-joke that Captain Janeway once mentioned a 'Planet Hell'. What with her other problems, you might expect her to avoid a place with a name like that. Well, guess what?

PLANET KILLER: Awesome extra-galactic weapon of destruction, so-called because it was able to carve up entire solar systems with its pure proton beam. It attacked the *Enterprise*, and not only did several people fall over, but a bit of smoke came out of the transporter pads.*

* *Which was pretty unlucky: with Captain Kirk stuck on the doomed Constellation, the thing most needed in good working order was the transporter system. It was fortuitous that they had the longest 20 seconds in history in which to repair them.*

PLANET OF TITANS: Proposed c. 1976 movie that was never made – obviously, else we'd have seen it. They did, however, get as far as designing a brand new, quite different, Starship *Enterprise* for it. This design was so good that, although it wasn't used for the main ship in any of the actual movies or subsequent TV series, a model of it was one of the ships destroyed at Wolf 359 in *Next Gen.*

PLAYMATES: Don't get too excited: in the world of *Star Trek*, this word has an entirely non-pornographic meaning. Specifically, Playmates are the purveyors of high quality action figures to the masses (Bandai repackage them for distribution in the UK and Europe) – and, being altruistic in nature, the company has taken it upon itself to go quite above and beyond the call of duty. We all know the problem: you're busy reconstructing classic Starfleet encounters in the privacy of your bedroom when your impromptu script unexpectedly calls for Geordi to be transformed into a Tarchannen III alien like he did in 'Identity Crisis'. It's happened to us all. But fear not, for now you can simply reach for the shelf and swap your bog-standard uniformed Geordi figure for one of him in his full metamorphosed glory. Never again will you have to simply pretend that Riker has been transformed into a Malcorian, nor that Picard has changed his clothes – you can make it so! And as for having to use one of your Will Riker figures to double as Thomas Riker . . . well, the very idea! What's more, Playmates kindly allow collectors to buy two copies of each figure: one to keep as mint and one to utterly devalue in the process of ripping open the packaging to get to the toy within. Some figures are individually numbered, which sounds great until you realise that the numbers have six digits, throwing into doubt your acquisition's status as a rare collector's piece.

PON FARR: Vulcan sexual rite, as described in 'Amok Time'. The interesting thing is, they have to do it every seven years or they'll snuff it. Oh yeah? Who thought up that one then? No doubt it was some ugly, big-eared inadequate who knew it was the only way he'd ever get a shag. As a chat-up technique, it's shamelessly exploitative: 'Quick, it's time for my Pon Farr – are you going to let me die or what?' But it really must have driven Spock round the twist, for why else would he have turned down Nurse Chapel on a plate in the hour of his greatest need? Of course, to the disappointment of some fans, neither did he look to Kirk for satisfaction. Instead, he plumped for a would-be bride whose idea of foreplay was to make him duel his best friend to the death so that she could cop off with someone else. Perhaps somebody needs to teach the Vulcans how to masturbate.

POSTER MAGAZINES: Several publishers have tried their hands at these, so there must be a few people out there with more money than sense. They pose a terrific dilemma for collectors, as they can hardly be kept in mint condition if you slap them up with a bit of blu-tack and wait for them to get ripped to shreds or fade – and if you don't do that, then what the hell is the point of buying them in the first place? It can't be for the token couple of facts that we all knew already on the reverse side, can it?

POWELL, JONATHAN: We had a bit of a go at him in our last book – but come on, this is the science fiction hating former BBC controller who quashed the hopes of the eager, *Star Trek* starved masses by announcing that the (then new) *The Next Generation* would never have a place on the BBC so long as he was in charge. Well, what a complete bastard, eh? Things have changed since his departure, of course: BBC2 aided our research for this book by screening *Voyager* on Sundays, *Next Gen* on Wednesdays, *DS9* on Thursdays and *TOS* on Fridays. And yet the legacy of Powell clearly lives on in the absence of a repeat broadcast for *The Animated Series*. Lucky we know them all off by heart, really.

POWERGEN: Recently nationalised electricity generating company in the UK. William Shatner and James Doohan appeared in a TV advert for shares. Shatner got to say the line 'Beam me up, Scotty' for once, but – for some reason that we've never quite worked out – was sent a brolly instead.

Hilarious. Well, about as funny as flogging off a publicly owned company, laying off a large proportion of the staff, and enabling directors and shareholders to make huge profits from rising fuel bills can be, anyway.

PRAVDA: Soviet newspaper which thought *Star Trek* was all right – for a capitalist American TV series, that is – but allegedly complained about the lack of a Russian character, leading to the inclusion of Pavel Chekov in the second season (talk about being careful of what you wish for). If you stop and really think about it, though, this oft-heard anecdote doesn't really hold water. Why would such a respectable publication beef about the casting of a low-budget, hardly popular (then), unregarded American science fiction TV show? Why would Americans, in the 1960s, give a toss if they did? The situation would be akin to a Chinese delegation complaining to Granada about the lack of oriental representation on *Coronation Street*. It comes as no surprise to learn from Walter Koenig, then, that the *Pravda* story is not true. It was a total lie, concocted as a publicity stunt. We feel betrayed.

PREGNANCY: Not uncommon among *Star Trek* regulars, surprisingly. So long as no sex is involved, of course: that would entail undesirable character development. Impregnation by aliens is probably the best cause, as that way the child can be conceived, gestated, born, grown up, and off the ship by the end of the episode. Surrogacy is a good fall-back should one of the regulars get up the duff in real life.

PRESIDENTS, DEAD: OK, so maybe outer space is teeming with wonders but, even in a science fiction TV series, the last thing you expect to see floating around out there is Abraham Lincoln in a comfy chair.

PRIME DIRECTIVE, THE: The Federation's non-interventionist policy relating to all non-aligned worlds. This stance must always be upheld even if it results in otherwise preventable loss of life. Lucky then that Kirk chose to ignore it most weeks. But really, it's a bit of a naff idea, isn't it? It only works one way, for a start. It's perfectly OK for the Vulcans to make first contact with us and to offer a leg-up into space, and when Kirk encountered Sargon his first thought was to get hold of all his lovely technological advances. On the other hand, if another race needs a bit of Starfleet help to, say, save themselves from extinction, they can just about sod off. An attempt to justify the Prime Directive occurred in 'Patterns of Force', when one John Gill learned that breaking the rules was not a good idea after all. But then, if you interpret 'interference with undeveloped cultures' as meaning 'taking over their world and refashioning it after Nazi Germany with yourself as its Fuhrer', then it wouldn't be.

PROBE SHIP: What James R Kirk claimed the *Enterprise* was in a pre-titles voice-over for the actual pilot form of 'Where No Man Has Gone Before'. Those whingers on *Voyager* reckon they're a long way from home but, in this version, the *Enterprise* is way beyond our galaxy. Far-fetched perhaps, but it kind of explains the title.

PSYCHO-KILLER ON BOARD: Funny how violent nutcase Suder, who'd been a *Voyager* crew member for almost two seasons, managed to remain unnoticed by his colleagues. If he hadn't had the sudden urge to smash someone's head in for looking at him in an annoying manner, he could have stayed undetected. Tuvok thought that a funny look was no logical motive for murder and went for an ill-advised mind meld, and what a rubbish serial killer he would have made following it. Naturally, he didn't kill anyone, but it was a good job no one else did, as the Vulcan was hardly behaving inconspicuously. 'Hmm, there's been another murder. I bet it was Tuvok: he keeps smashing the furniture up, insulting the captain and saying he wants to kill someone.'

PSYCHO-TRICORDER: Specialist item of equipment carried by Lt. Karen Tracey. It must have been knackered however, because it failed to detect the psycho who murdered her. (Who may or may not have been Mr Scott – see JACK THE RIPPER.)

PULASKI, KATE: Replacement doctor in *TNG* season two. We thought she was fine (well, apart from her hairdo). However, despite Diana Muldaur's pedigree,* unforgiving fans couldn't accept her taking over from their beloved Dr Beverly Crusher. Though they somehow found it in their hearts to forgive Bev for giving birth to Wesley Crusher.

*As well as appearing as different doctors in two TOS episodes, she starred in Planet Earth, one of two near-identical Gene Roddenberry pilots set in a post-apocalyptic future. Or was she in Genesis II (the other one)? Anyway, she was in the one that didn't have Mariette Hartley from 'All Our Yesterdays' as the female lead.

Q

Q: One of several near-omnipotent beings who have taken it upon themselves to test Federation members, for no apparent reason, at one time or another but especially during pilot episodes. Unlike the others, John de Lancie's extra-dimensional character was a big hit and has now appeared in three *Star Trek* strands (with a movie début imminent). Writers cottoned on to the punning potential of using his name in episode titles, but too late to do much about 'Encounter at Farpoint'. 'QPid' and 'Deja Q' are both laudable examples of silly appellations, and *DS9*'s 'Q-Less' is OK. But whoever thought up 'Hide and Q' really missed the point. They do this sort of thing less often nowadays, going for mundane stuff like 'All Good Things' and 'Death Wish' instead; can't think why, as the possibilities are far from exhausted.

TEN GREAT TITLES WAITING TO BE USED FOR Q STORIES

1: Q Gardens. He takes up horticulture.

2: Q Cumber. The continuation. Q uses his powers to encourage the growth of his new crops, but loses control and ends up with a giant comedy vegetable.

3: B & Q. He does it himself, in a story so good you have to tell someone (apologies to American readers: you won't get this one).

4: 4Q. His fourth story. Obviously.

5: Miss Q. Oh, what a missed opportunity! They do an

157

episode about a woman from the Q continuum and what do they call it? 'True Q'. Well, we ask you!

6: Thank Q. Likewise, Picard shows his gratitude at last and they plump for 'Tapestry'. Why oh why use such a dull name when this corker's lined up in the wings?

7: Q Tips. Q has a cup of tea. Guest starring Paul Young.

8: Q Wait. He doesn't appear for the duration of the episode . . .

9: Bus Q . . . then four of him turn up at once.

10: Barbie Q. He becomes a living doll. Alternatively, this would be a great follow up to our favourite piece of *Star Trek* merchandise (see BARBIE AND KEN).

QO'NOS: Something tells us that the *Star Trek* producers got their priorities wrong when they created a comprehensive language structure for the Klingon race and yet neglected to give their home world a proper and consistent name. 'The Klingon homeworld' was favourite for a time, though now they've finally bitten the bullet and pretty much established that it's Qo'noS (or Kronos in 'Federation Standard'). So what was wrong with *The Original Series*'s first effort, Kling?

QUADRANTS: Naturally, there are four of these nowadays. However, there were loads of them in *The Original Series*: presumably because someone didn't know what the word meant.

QUANTUM TORPEDOES: The latest weaponry, fitted aboard the *Defiant* and the Sovereign Class *Enterprise E*, because obviously there can't be a Starfleet ship with more firepower than the *Enterprise* (and wouldn't you know it, *Voyager* even managed to find some in the delta quadrant), all in all, an, erm, quantum leap in technology.

QUCH: The Klingon word for 'forehead', so the literal translation is probably something like 'embarrassing brown lump', but with more aggressive overtones. For some reason, mis-shapen foreheads have taken the place of proper costumes in *Star Trek*, the latter having been used in *The Original Series* to create such classic monsters as Korob, the Mugato and that ape-thing from Taurus II. Hmm, come to think of it, we can see why now. But the modern-day Klingon domes have presented satirists with a problem: everyone agrees that they resemble an item of confectionery, but there seems to be some dispute as to which it is. So, in the interests of strict accuracy, let us examine all the evidence. Hmm, well, we'd have to say that Worf is the most famous of Klingons, and the great protruding ridge down the centre of his forehead certainly does look like a cornish pastie. Indeed, his slightly redesigned look after *Next Gen* season one only reinforced the pastry crust image. But then, many different cranial designs are in use to represent the Klingon forehead, and most of these are somewhat less bulgy. Their complexion, too, seems to favour that other main contender: the Mars bar (or the Milky Way, as they'd call it in the States – just thought we'd bring our American friends in on the joke there). It also has to be said that this latter option offers a possible explanation for the lumpless appearance of *The Original Series*'s Klingons, which Worf found so embarrassing in 'Trials and Tribble-ations': the chocolate melted. So which one to employ? Well, we thought long and hard about the problem before deciding to use both interchangeably, for maximum piss-taking opportunity. By the way, has anyone noticed how the back of a Ferengi's head looks an awful lot like an arse?

QUESTOR: Android star of *The Questor Tapes*: another of Gene Roddenberry's attempts to repeat the success of *Star Trek*. He revived and renamed the character to become Data in *Next Gen* – and, as if to prove that new ideas were not necessary for his new show, went on to base Riker and Troi on Decker and Ilia from *Star Trek II/The Motion Picture*. (See *STAR TREK II*.)

QUINTOTRITICALE: Future refinement of the grain triticale, which helped stave off a famine on Sherman's Planet. Oh yes it did: they might have used the comparatively primitive quadrotriticale in 'The Trouble with Tribbles', but the Federation had gone one better by the time of the lovable fuzzballs' second appearance in 'More Tribbles, More Troubles'. This sort of attention to detail is unusual, if not unique, in an animated spin-off. So why didn't Gene bloody Roddenberry just admit that the cartoon episodes were canonical? We despair.

R

RAYNA: Sexy blonde android who was yet another attempt at creating the perfect woman, so naturally she fell in love with Kirk. Sadly, prolonged exposure to his overacting caused her to short circuit. However, even with this unfortunate design fault, she was a sight more impressive than her robotic chum M-4, who looked like it had been constructed with left-over cooking utensils from a Chinese restaurant.

REDWOOD, JOHN: Tory politician and regular leadership contender, often compared to a Vulcan by his enemies (i.e., other Tory politicians). However, he has taken pains to shake off his humourless image; indeed, his off-the-cuff, mid-soundbite quips are just as amusing as Spock's witty end-of-the-episode one-liners. Out of all his party members, Redwood at least has the best excuse for when he is caught in the inevitable sex scandal. (See PON FARR for details.)

'REMEMBER ME': Remember how Anita Dobson put lyrics to the *EastEnders* theme and had a smashing hit single a few years back? Well Gene Roddenberry beat her to it by about two decades, with just as much artistic success, when he fitted words to *The Original Series* music (though thankfully he didn't try to get the results into the charts). Like Anita, he chose to write a soppy song about unrequited love and all that sentimental balls, with some woman moaning about her partner being far away in space and easy prey for exotic alien temptresses ('His star trek will go on forever'). It concluded with the words 'remember me' – and, by way of a clever in-joke, *Next Gen* later did an episode called

'Remember Me' in their fourth season. So there you go, another fascinating fact.

'RESISTANCE IS FUTILE': Just because the Borg are an emotionless collective without any concept of individuality doesn't mean they can't have a catch-phrase. They are *Star Trek* characters after all! Their now-familiar mantra also became the tag-line for *First Contact*, their first big-screen appearance. Yes, how imaginative it is, and how carefully it avoids comparison with that entirely dissimilar phrase which has now become a dull science fiction cliché: 'Resistance is useless.'

RESURRECTION: A working title for the eighth *Star Trek* film, which ultimately became *First Contact*. They changed it when it was revealed that *Aliens 4* was considering using a similar name but, more importantly, when they realised that everyone was (and still is) expecting Kirk's return and that they were sort of suggesting it would happen. Still, they could have gone for something more original than an existing *Next Gen* episode title. But if they were bothered about such things, we suppose they wouldn't have named *The Final Frontier* after a novel by Diane Carey, nor *Deep Space Nine*'s pilot episode, 'The Emissary', after *Next Gen*'s slightly snappier 'Emissary'. We know there's a finite number of words in the English language, but really . . .

RIKER, THOMAS: He's a lot like William Riker – identical actually, except he's got a bit of an attitude thanks to being left in some crap hole for years following the transporter accident that created him. For some reason, he also looks a lot thinner. The fact that either or both of them could be the original ought to be a bit worrying for regular transporter users – what's to say it doesn't really work like a sophisticated photocopier, killing whoever gets into it during the energy conversion process, then simply creating a clever duplicate? No wonder Barclay and McCoy are scared of the things. Phew, lucky they're only a far-fetched, scientifically impossible SF concept, really.

RISA: Famed pleasure planet and subject of much raised-eyebrow innuendo in *The Next Generation*. It disappointed a little when we finally saw it and it turned out to be just a bog-standard place with some sun, sand and trees. *Deep Space Nine* added the sex, as it so often does, and showed us a world on which natives and visitors alike are permanently horny as hell and even Quark can cop off at the shake of a stick. In other words, Risa (Riser more like) is the 24th-century equivalent of a Club 18–30 holiday, perhaps named for its effect upon certain organs. So, naturally, at the time of the *DS9* crew's visit, a bunch of puritans were demonstrating about the evil consequences of having too much fun. Isn't that just typical? Another scourge of society still active in the so-called Utopian future. They'll probably still be showing cut versions of 'Conspiracy' in 500 years' time, too.

RIVA: Despite looking like he'd be more at home as one of the Bee Gees, he was a legendary mediator. He was also deaf (quite an advantage when in the Bee Gees) and therefore had need of a chorus of telepathic interpreters. Riva really fancied Deanna Troi, and attempted to use one of his translators to chat her up. For some reason Deanna didn't relish the idea of a threesome and chose instead to use her own remarkable powers to communicate directly with her bearded suitor. Well, she got there eventually, but whatever you do, don't play charades with this woman unless you've got a fortnight to spare.

RIZZO: One of three red-shirted crew members killed by a smokey alien. Kirk seemed unusually concerned by this – and it wasn't as if any of his blue-mini-dressed female crewmates had bought it – and decided to go after the foggy fiend, giving it the opportunity to thrash a couple more blokes in red. We should have realised, however, that Kirk wasn't too fussed about the easily replaced casualties: he was actually hell-bent on vengeance because he was bitter about his failure to wipe out the creature eleven years earlier. Never mind, second time lucky eh?

ROCKS: Strangely, with the notable exception of the ones that turn out to be silicon-based life forms, these appear remarkably similar on all the planets visited by the original *Enterprise* crew. The versatility of these oft-used props* was sometimes enhanced by having Captain Kirk leap athletically over one of them, when it would have been just as easy to walk around it (see the climactic ending of 'Who Mourns for Adonais' for a particularly impressive leap).

* *Former Doctor Who Sylvester McCoy (no relation) claims to have written fan letters to one of Star Trek's rocks; we don't know if he ever received a reply.*

ROM: Ferengi character resident on *Deep Space Nine* and clearly named after the '70s space-knight of cheap toy/tie-in Marvel comic fame (see X-MEN for his other uncanny link with *Star Trek*). This could be passed off as a coincidence were it not for the fact that Rom's brother is called Quark, no doubt after the ferocious mechanical race seen in television's *Doctor Who* during the late '60s. Clearly, the Ferengi's parents were great fans of late 20th-century science fiction robots. We eagerly await the episode in which another sibling, 7-Zark-7, pays a visit to the station.

ROMAINE, LT. MIRA: Mr Scott's girlfriend – he loved her almost as much as the *Enterprise*'s engines. Yet he never saw her again after she'd had 100 Zetarians inside her. Funny, that.

ROMULANS: It was established early on that this race was closely related to the Vulcans, thus the appearance of both races was identical in *The Original Series*. Yet what happens when *Next Gen* comes along? The producers suddenly decide to stick lumpy bits on their heads. What is it with these guys and knobbly craniums?

ROZHENKO, NIKOLAI: Worf's sort of foster brother. They are very unalike (and not just because Nicky hasn't got a lumpy head), but obviously he's brilliant and a natural leader – because it's not allowed for relatives of *Star Trek* regulars to be traffic wardens or anything less than fantastic. Much to the disgust of all aboard the *Enterprise D*, Nikolai committed the ultimate sin – a gross violation of the Prime Directive – by attempting to save the lives of some of the inhabitants of a culturally rich world otherwise doomed to destruction. What a complete and utter evil bastard.

'RULES OF LUTON, THE': Episode of *Space: 1999* with a less-than-exotic-sounding location and a plot remarkably similar to that of 'Arena' (starring the fantastic Gorn). Come to think of it though, before Trekkies start labelling the Anderson show 'derivative', that *TOS* adventure was recycled from a 1944 short story by Frederick Brown published in *Astounding Science Fiction* entitled, erm, 'The Arena' (try and hide the fact guys, why don't you?). Oh yes, and *The Outer Limits* episode 'Fun and Games' was pretty similar too.*

* *So was* Star Trek*'s own 'Savage Curtain'.***
** *And of course 'Spectre of the Gun' too, although that one had a Wild West setting to try and disguise its roots.*

S

SAFE SEX: Practised by Captain Kirk it seems, otherwise the galaxy would be littered with his progeny. There was a close call with Miramanee, but, as far as we are aware, Kirk's only offspring is David Marcus, who was tragically killed by Klingon bastards.

SALT VAMPIRE: By appearing in 'The Man Trap', broadcast on 8 September 1966, this alien had the privilege of being the first encountered on the five-, er, three-year mission, and not even the fact that the episodes weren't shown in the intended order can change this. Naturally the creature also holds the distinction of being the first one to be utterly wiped out by Kirk and his buddies. OK, so maybe she killed a few people, but a girl's gotta eat.

SASH, WORF'S: How come Worf's allowed to wear this deviation from regular Starfleet get-up? And more to the point, why does he wear it? Maybe he won a beauty contest once. Perhaps that would explain why he's taken to wearing that stupid pig-tail. Hardened Klingon warrior? Give it up, mate, you look like a big girl's blouse.

SATAN: Popular historical figure. When they first got a glimpse of Spock, studio executives – who are notoriously thick – thought he looked like Old Nick. Possibly recalling this incident, 'The Apple' saw Kirk hinting that someone aboard the *Enterprise* resembled Satan. Although knowing full well that he meant him, Spock feigned ignorance* – perhaps inwardly saying to himself, 'Look you baldy git, have I got horns and a pointy tail? No. And if I did have a pitchfork I'd stick it right up your fat arse.' Or perhaps not.

* *Actually Spock is suspiciously well-informed about Satan's activities in 'Catspaw'. Hmm, food for thought there.*

'SAVAGE CURTAIN, THE': Irresponsibly titled episode of *The Original Series*. Impressionable children might get to see it and become afraid that their drapes were about to leap off the windows and attack them.

SCOTT, MONTGOMERY: The first *Enterprise*'s fatalistic chief engineer. The man was constantly suffering from the delusion that his engines were not up to the task for which they were designed, and, indeed, were about to explode at any moment. A clear case of paranoia; Scotty really ought to consider counselling.

SECOND FROM TOP: Position held by Bashir in his class, at the time of his graduation. Hold on a mo, that can't be right. How did he get into *Star Trek* if he's not perfect? It might be *Deep Space Nine*, but, even so, this is an unacceptable flaw in his character. Fortunately, the writers noticed and ret-conned it so that Bashir cocked up his final exam on purpose. We're still not sure why, though.

SEPTEMBER 8TH*: A red-letter day to be sure, for it's the date on which, in 1973, *The Animated Series* premièred. Oh yeah, almost forgot, *The Original Series* débuted on the same date too, in 1966.

* *Coincidentally, September 8th also happens to be the birthday of one of the authors (the one with the initials CH) of this 'ere book. All prezzies c/o Virgin please (no Trek memorabilia, though).*

SESKA: It takes a brave and innovative series to have one of its regular cast members turn bad and not get rehabilitated by the end of the episode. A pity then that *Voyager* copped out and opted for a character who had appeared only a couple of times and looked pretty shady anyway. Much better if they'd bitten the bullet and maybe had Chakotay go mad and scalp everyone because his animal spirit-guide told him to, or let Neelix cook up the crew in a yummy big casserole. But when they wanted another of the ship's crew to join Seska, who did they choose? Paris, as was strongly hinted? Her old friend, Torres? Nope. Janeway was betrayed by . . . Michael Jonas. Who?

SEX: Is there something in the water on *Deep Space Nine* or what? Those fans who were upset by the constantly salacious nature of *The Next Generation* (see the footnote to 'GET A LIFE!' and, in fact, those fans should read 'GET A LIFE!' too) must have had apoplexies when Dax and Worf started pawing each other, Quark trapped off with a Klingon and O'Brien and Kira fought to keep each other at arm's length lest they accidentally shag – and that was just in one episode! Add to this Bashir's new ability to pull birds left, right and centre (his 'separation ritual' from Leeta seemed, for some reason, to involve lots of kissing and touching with several people) and the whole issue of Kira's pregnancy . . . and some characters (Sisko, Kira, Bashir, Garak) have even managed to find partners who are still around by the end of their first episode and who come back for more! It's hardly like *Star Trek* at all. In fact, did anyone else notice that Sisko's mirror universe opposite was a dead ringer, personality-wise, for Captain Kirk? This became more than clear when our Sisko had to impersonate him: Trill, Bajoran or human, if it had tits he'd hump it. At this rate, they'll be renaming the show *Deep Throat Nine*. Or perhaps *Deep Space Sixty-Nine*. Oh well then, please yourselves.

SEXISM: Allegation laid against the fourth season of *Deep Space Nine* by fans, just because former terrorist Kira Nerys suddenly took to slinking about the station with a spray-on costume and high heels, attracting the lascivious attentions of all about her. And yet those same fans have been complaining for yonks that *DS9* isn't similar enough to *The Original*

Series. Surely a spot of blatant debasement of women is a step in the right direction?

SHIP OF DEATH, THE: Affectionate nickname by which *Voyager* is known in certain places where its reputation has preceded it. Come to think of it, why don't they find out who's been spreading these rumours and borrow their ship – it's obviously a lot faster.

SHIRTS, RED: Everyone who beamed down to a planet's surface in one of these, etc., etc. You all know the story and it's blindingly obvious in every episode of *The Original Series* if you don't. Fans who watched the first instalment of *Next Gen* in agonising suspense, wondering if it would be faithful to the spirit of its predecessor, were comforted by the pre-titles sequence in which Q casually murdered a red-garbed extra and tradition was maintained. Presumably, certain members of Starfleet personnel eventually cottoned on to this and refused to leave the ship or, in Decker and Ilia's case in *The Motion Picture*, took to wearing other colours in the hope of cheating fate. They couldn't cheat the writers, though, who knew they weren't central cast members and slayed them accordingly. Now under the misapprehension that red shirts weren't jinxed at all, Starfleet introduced burgundy uniforms across the board; however, the loss of several *Enterprises* in rapid succession saw to it that a range of multi-coloured replacements was swiftly brought in. (See also DEATH SEAT.)

SHORT SKIRTS: Yet another concession to sexual equality: if the women on the *Enterprise* had to wear those tiny things that covered their modesty only providing they remained perfectly still, then the men had to have skirts too. And those silly things at the bottom of their trousers were surely just as embarrassing as anything their female shipmates were required to wear.

TEN FEMALE CREWMEMBERS OF THE ORIGINAL *ENTERPRISE* WHO SHOWED THEIR PANTS

1: Flippin' 'eck, they all did.

SIDDIG, ALEXANDER: Brilliant actor who replaced Siddig El Fadil as Dr Julian Bashir in *DS9*. In fact he's so good you can hardly tell it's a different bloke.

SIDDIG, ALEXANDER (addendum): Blimey, don't we feel stupid? Apparently it is the same bloke, and he just changed his name. Dunno why, though obviously Alexander is a great name (think about it).

***SIMPSONS, THE*:** Usually amusing cartoon series which often features bizarre yellow caricatures of celebrities. It once looked to the *Star Trek* movies for source material and came to the hilarious conclusion that Kirk was a bit past it and Scotty was overweight. An example of observational comedy, no doubt.

SIR: Term by which even female officers are usually addressed in Starfleet, which concerns us greatly as surely even the most alien race can tell, say, Kira Nerys from Benjamin Sisko (though Sisko himself still has to learn that Dax isn't an 'old man')? It is based on the current status quo in the US armed forces and suggests that, even by the 24th century, a woman in a high-ranking position is a bit of an oddity. But if they were to change it, it might be seen as a hint that the Americans won't be calling the shots in space in 500 years' time, which would never do.

SKULL CAP: There are some interesting photos of Persis

Khambatta, in Ilia mode from the unmade *Star Trek II*, sporting one of these to appear bald. But, for her appearance in *The Motion Picture* they must have offered sufficient, er, inducement for her to go for it and get her head shaved good and proper. Unusual for a *Star Trek* movie that, someone trying to look bald who isn't . . .

SLASH FICTION: Term applied by fandom to those homespun yarns in which Kirk and Spock get it together. Perhaps we haven't been paying attention, as we've somehow missed the constant sexual tension which obviously smoulders between these two characters. But why is it called 'slash fiction', we wonder? Because its perpetrators deserve to be eviscerated with a sharp blade? Or, on a more colloquial level, is it just so we can take the piss out of it? (See also *TEXTUAL POACHERS*.)

SLOW-MOTION PICTURE, THE: See *MOTIONLESS PICTURE, THE*.

SPACE HIPPIES: Group encountered by Kirk and his crew in 'The Way to Eden'. This was *Star Trek*'s attempt to be hip and relevant for the '60s but, coming as it did in the third season of *TOS*, it was just embarrassing. The seekers of paradise were led by a character called Adam – as they are wont to be in these analogies – and were distressingly keen to drop into songs about brotherhood and peace at the slightest provocation. But what's worse is that Spock saw fit to join them, thus showing once and for all why Vulcans are taught to keep a tight rein on their emotions. It's to stop them from looking like dickheads.

SPACE TALK SERIES: Sub-division of Playmates/ Bandai's never-ending series of *Star Trek* models which, along with yet more models of Picard and co. (see 1,701) – each equipped to utter genuine clichés from the series – features a foot-long model of the *Enterprise D*. This is programmed with a claimed 100 phrases, although in practice these consist of various combinations of significantly fewer words ('photon torpedoes', 'tractor beams', 'engaged', etc). Still, it's a lovely chintzy bit of memorabilia and pretty accurate, but for one flaw. Alas, that flaw is quite a major logistical one, which should have been spotted at an early stage ... THE *ENTERPRISE* CAN'T TALK!!!

SPANKING: Old Earth custom that Kirk was familiar with. He threatened its use on spoilt bitch Elaan; her enthusiastic response suggested she was familiar with the practice too.

SPOCK, DOCTOR: Author of several books on child psychology; not to be confused with *Star Trek*'s Mr Spock – though he often is.

SPOCK, MISTER: As a member of the dispassionate Vulcan race, the original *Enterprise*'s science officer has been bred so as to be incapable of having illogical feelings. He thus approaches every situation in a totally ordered, rational and humourless manner. Except, that is, for when the end of an episode is looming, at which point it becomes permissible for him to crack a few gags and to raise his eyebrow suggestively towards camera when Doctor McCoy comments upon the possibility of emotions stirring in that cold Vulcan heart of his. (See also CUSTOMARY JOKE AT THE END OF THE EPISODE.)

SPOON HEADS: The Bajorans' nicknames for their Cardassian occupiers, apparently. Very apposite we're sure, and it's what we were all thinking anyway, but shouldn't the writers be briefed not to call attention to such things? That's why no one in *The Original Series* ever said, 'That alien's dressed in tin foil, Jim' or, 'Ooh, look, there's that rock again.' What next? We can just imagine the scene as Dax enters Quark's Bar:

> 'Give us a drink, Bum Head.'
> 'Get one yourself, Spotty – Crap Nose has closed me down again.'
> 'But I'm meeting Pastie Face here later . . .' etc., etc.

SQUARED PAPER: What you'd have 144 sheets of if you splashed out and bought the *Star Trek: The Next Generation* journal from Antioch. Well, they call it a journal; however, it doesn't have any of the contents one might associate with such a thing (words, etc.). It's nice squared paper though, and according to the cover sticker it's 'bound to lie flat'; that is, it's a hardback. But here's the really good bit: it has a big picture of the *Enterprise* on its front. Perhaps not an ideal collector's piece, especially at £7.99, but if you're a would-be draughtsman as well as an ardent Trekkie it will provide hours of fun (so long as you don't use it, of course, as this would ruin its value). What's more, if your graph paper fetish isn't assuaged yet, you can fork out another eight quid for – you've guessed it – the *Star Trek: Deep Space Nine* journal. In fact, these products exist for every incarnation of the franchise, bar one (guess which). There are also similar, smaller versions on the market, in which costs have been slashed and prices lowered by the removal of vertical lines.

STARBASES: There are over 700 of these. Notable examples include Starbase 12, Starbase 73, Starbase 105, and who can forget Starbase 218?

STARCHASER: Britain's very own space programme which has enhanced its credibility by using *Star Trek*-style lettering in its logo. Based up the road from us, in Didsbury, the Starchaser Foundation boasts a fleet of four rockets, including *Starchaser 1B*, a three-metre, 121-kilogram replacement for *Starchaser 1A*. Blimey, 1A and 1B! They're getting more like Starfleet all the time. Another *Star Trek*-inspired British-based space project was that belonging to Barry from Emmerdale, who planned to blast Butch Dingle off into space in a pig muck-powered rocket. The *Trek* influence was evident from the model *Enterprise* Barry had stuck on the barn wall.

STARDATES: Initially brought in to make *Star Trek* look all futuristic, these were really a bad idea. Why would any enlightened civilisation abandon a perfectly logical system of time measurement for a supposedly linear one which, in practice, fluctuates alarmingly, sometimes in the course of a single day? And, apart from in the log entries of various captains, when are they ever mentioned? We don't hear people asking 'What day is it today?' and being told '3.2'. Of course, there was that bit in *The Original Series* when Kirk claimed to someone's face that Starfleet didn't count in seconds, but this was clearly just an irresponsible prank on his part. Anyway, what is a 'stardate' supposed to be exactly? How can we take any incarnation of *Star Trek* seriously when its plausibility is undermined in such a basic manner?

STARFLEET ACADEMY: The place where precocious, young irritating cadets or – and let's call a spade a spade here – students hang out, no doubt imbibing copious amounts of subsidised synth-ale. Thankfully, the college and its inhabitants feature very infrequently in televised exploits, but there are both paperback and comic book series,* as well as a range of action figures. These, we feel, should be regarded as the *Star Trek* franchise's equivalent of, say, *Tiny Toons* or *Muppet Babies*.**

* Marvel's comic book series features Nog. One minute he's telling Sisko he wants to join the Academy, the next he's in the comic; which is fine for readers, not perhaps so good for the actor who plays him in DS9. Also in the line-up are Matt Decker (probably some relation), a female Andorian – who appeared naked in the first issue, but because of the comics code authority, you didn't see her tits or anything – and some others, but who cares?
** Though, come to think of it, The Animated Series *featured a similar concept years before either of these appeared.*

STAR JOURNEY: Dead clever name for a couple of space-related documentary videos, released by Merlin and narrated by William Shatner and Patrick Stewart but having nothing to do with *Star Trek* whatsoever, honest. As if we'd even think it.

STAR TREK MEMORIES: Yet another autobiography by a crew member from *The Original Series*, and isn't it great that they all turned out to be such talented writers. This one was

William Shatner's first attempt to explain himself and it's notable primarily because, in the course of researching it, he found out what the rest of the cast thought of him.* He can't have read their own autobiographies then, else he'd have known already. It got to the point when fans would rush out to buy each new book, just to see how much 'Shatner-bashing' it contained. *Star Trek Memories*, incidentally, was ghost-written by Chris Kreski, whose previous credits included scripts for *Beavis and Butt-Head*. You can tell.

* *He also penned a follow-up,* Star Trek Movie Memories, *and no doubt discovered they still didn't like him when making the films.*

STAR TREK: NEW FRONTIER: It seems that the umpteen *Star Trek* novels churned out every month aren't enough to satisfy the voracious reading appetites of those Trekkies whose obsession only allows them to read books if they feature Starfleet vessels, Klingons, etc.* Hence this series of paperback adventures set aboard the USS *Excalibur* with Captain Calhoun and his crew, some of whom are obscure characters from various *Next Gen* episodes (admittedly both Shelby and Selar were pretty fanciable on screen, but this hardly transfers well to the printed page). Unfortunately for the less obsessed fans, they're penned by a decent writer, Peter David, so there may be a temptation to buy them. Though we suppose this might present a good excuse to drop the other titles from the shopping list for a while.

* *Though, following episodes like 'Elementary, Dear Data' and 'Time's Arrow', maybe they're able to try perusing a little Conan Doyle or Mark Twain without feeling too guilty.*

STAR TREK NIGHT: Misnomer for BBC2's weekend-long *Star Trek* extravaganza of 1996. Blimey, who'd have thought it? After years of denying the popularity of science fiction (and of not making any!) the BBC decided to pull out all the stops to mark *Trek*'s 30th anniversary. Or perhaps they just wanted to deride it, as their pick of episodes for the so-called celebration was not quite inspired ('Encounter at Farpoint', 'The Caretaker', something from *The Original Series*, etc.).

Diehard fans were reportedly upset by the accompanying irreverent documentaries too, which included the imaginatively titled 'Funk Me Up Scotty' (mocking all those crappy records that we too mocked a few sections back) and the even more inspired 'Spoof Trek' which, in attempting to show how amusing most skits on the programme are, sadly accomplished the opposite. Never mind, the Beeb's *Radio Times Official Collector's Edition* was unusually excellent, despite the omission of a complete episode guide to *The Animated Series*. Perhaps this was because it was written in the USA by people who knew what they were talking about: the dead giveaway is that some sections have been personalised for what Americans would imagine to be the delight of UK readers. The sample Klingonese phrases are the most telling, betraying the belief that we just want to ask 'Spot of tea?', talk about Lady Di and cricket, and say 'bloody' a lot.* Bad show, you jolly rotters!

* *Which admittedly we do in this book, but only because Virgin won't let us say f***. See!*

***STAR TREK SKETCH BOOK*:** A terribly disappointing publication, this. There we were expecting a hilarious collection of comedy scripts featuring stuck-on pointed ears and ladies' compacts, etc., and what should be in it but drawings of the *Enterprise*, its bridge and suchlike. Where's the point in that?

***STAR TREK: THE MOTION PICTURE* ORIGINAL FILM CELLS:** Alleged collectors' items. Perhaps the idea is to buy thousands of them (at hilarious prices) and splice them together into the complete movie. If so, wouldn't it be cheaper just to buy the video?

***STAR TREK II*:** It must have been awful being a *Star Trek* fan in the mid-70s, living only for repeats, *The Animated Series* and a daily letter of protest about the show's cancellation. Perhaps Paramount didn't know what they had created – *Star Trek* fans, that is, not the series itself. Or perhaps they did, but hoped it would go away. It didn't – and eight years into a concerted campaign, the company surrendered at last. The imaginatively titled *Star Trek II** made it onto the drawing-board: a new run of episodes, featuring the original characters and one or two extras. Then, frustration of frustrations, it was scrapped. Seems they realised it might look a bit crap next to the newly released *Star Wars*. In retrospect, this was a kindness, as no SF TV show ever gained credibility from having been made in the '70s. And anyway, from its ashes rose *The Motion Picture*, based on a completed, unused script (and giving us a glimpse of what the already-cast Decker and Ilia would have been like too, before they were summarily despatched). 'In Thy Image' would have been a great 50-minute episode, so what a shame it ran for over two hours. This didn't stop psycho fans from demanding the reinstatement of scenes that were pruned before release – perhaps they were at a loose end without their daily protest letters to write. Oh yes, and a couple more *Star Trek II* scripts turned up as *Next Gen*'s 'The Child' and 'Devil's Due', modified of course for the new crew. That's why Picard uncharacteristically copped off in the latter. Nice to know some things were never destined to change. (See also XON.)

* *Or should it officially be known as* Star Trek Phase II? *The only real advantage of this would be to avoid confusion with* The Wrath of Khan; *in all other respects it doesn't matter a jot. Surely the most important thing is that they didn't make the bloody series.*

STATING THE BLEEDIN' OBVIOUS: One of Deanna Troi's two major character flaws. Yes, what a lot of use she'd be in a fully fledged war. While the rest of the crew were wading knee-deep in blood, desperately fighting for their lives and being cut down by marauding Klingons or whatever, she'd be the one saying, 'Captain, I sense great hostility.' Still, her colleagues have put up with this gladly since the events of 'The Loss' showed them what a complete and utter bitch Troi was without her so-called powers. Her other vice is a self-confessed addiction to chocolate, so her attraction to the *Enterprise*'s Klingon officer is not surpising. Look out, Worf mate, she's only after you for your Mars bar!

STRATOS: *Flash Gordon*esque floating city in *TOS*'s 'The Cloud Minders', and just the kind of thing people would have been quick to slag off had it appeared in *The Animated Series*. Presumably it was called Stratos because it was a bit near to the stratosphere. Clever, eh?

'SUB ROSA': Unintentionally hilarious episode set on Caldos IV where the colonists are of Scots descent – seemingly straight from Brigadoon. Klingons are well advised to avoid this planet, given that deep-fried Mars bars are a popular Scottish delicacy.

SUGAR SMACKS: Breakfast cereal for the sweet-toothed that had quite a plethora of free badges for a while, including sets featuring *Captain Scarlet*, *Joe 90*, *Doctor Who*, and of course *Star Trek*. Best of these, featuring box-front star Mr Spock et al., was the Starfleet insignia one. When worn on a mustard-coloured jersey it felt just like being Captain Kirk himself; especially with the addition of one of the cardboard cut-out masks from the back of the cereal packet.

TEN HIGHLIGHTS OF THE DEVOTED TREKKIE'S DAY

1: 'The USS *Voyager* is 70,000 light years from home and we are desperate to get back. Are you going to lie there all day?' Of course you aren't; not after such a rousing wake-up call from your Wesco *Star Trek: Voyager* clock. But you'll have to hit the snooze button anyway just to hear it say, 'Attention all those in sleeping quarters: move now or be left behind!' Then you're ready to don your Starfleet uniform and face the day.

2: Breakfast. It's been a while since any cereal was sanctioned by the *Star Trek* franchise (in the UK, that is, but you could always send off for some Canadian Cornflakes) and your Sugar Smacks are a bit crusty.

Even your Weetabix, with their free *Motion Picture* stand-up cards, are frayed at the edges. Still, you have dozens of boxes of each left (it took you a few tries to get full sets of all the giveaways) and you have to show your gratitude to the manufacturers somehow. So put on your Kirk mask and get chewing. You can always wash it down with some prune juice.

3: Some shopping, perhaps. It wouldn't do to miss the release date of any merchandise. And it's a chance to use that Bank of Scotland credit card, with its beautiful and not-at-all-sad picture of the *Enterprise D* engaging warp speed. Better yet, whip out your *Next Generation* chequebook. You may suffer a small amount of ridicule as you pay for your *Official Star Trek Monthly* with a picture of Jean-Luc Picard or someone, filling in a stardate and signing above a line of pithy wisdom such as 'Make it so', but you know it's a cool thing to do. Whatever, if you find yourself writing cheques for gold-pressed latinum, there's no hope.

4: Lunchtime is ideal for some light viewing: perhaps one of the umpteen documentaries, or better yet, your own appearance in the *Star Trek Adventure*, filmed at Universal Studios. There you are, dressed in Starfleet uniform (so no change there) and operating controls on the *Enterprise* bridge (without actually touching them, strangely). By now, you can recite the script along with yourself as you beam across to the Klingon vessel for the proudest moment of your 'life'.

5: Since the arrival of the internet, you have a full and varied social life. You can log on and spend a few hours downloading and sending pithy comments about the merits or otherwise of the latest *Voyager* episode, which film was the best and whether *Star Wars* fans are sadder than you.

6: Time for a spot of reading. The latest offering from Pocket Books will do: pick up the next one in sequence from the teetering mound of unread publications that has built up over the years. You race through the pages, speed-reading, desperate to reach the end before ... oops, too late. They've released another four.

7: It's tea time, so lay out your 'Best of Both Worlds' plates, dig out *The Official Star Trek Fact Files* and get to work on a banana split. Something to drink? No problem, with your lovely decanter in the shape of Mr Spock's head and shoulders. If you can fill it with something green, it's just like tearing off the Vulcan's head and letting his blood drip into your cup.

8: Unwind for a couple of hours with the *Star Trek* crew. Or rather, with your complete collection of mega-expensive, life-size cardboard cut-outs, but it's as near as you'll get. Pour yourself a drink and circulate, exchanging pleasantries with the cream of Starfleet. Just like being on deck ten forward.

9: Almost bedtime and you can climb into your specially made pyjamas, patterned, of course, after the uniforms in *The Motion Picture* (your official Funantics *Next Gen* kids' pyjamas don't fit any more, no matter how you diet) and lay out your *Star Trek* sleeping bag and Mr Spock teddy bear. But before you can retire:

10: Check that your video timer worked and that the day's episodes have been successfully recorded from BBC2 and Sky. Scrutinise the new off-air copies to see if they're of better quality than your last off-air copies. Keep both anyway, just in case. Label the new tapes and file them in chronological order of original broadcast dates (in the case of *The Original Series*, of course you'll have to keep one set in the alternative, but more sensible, production order too). Then set the video for tomorrow. Who knows? One day you might even find the time to watch some of this stuff.

SUICIDE MISSIONS: These come along every so often, giving Starfleet members the chance to jeopardise their lives by boldly going to a place from which they are unlikely to return (but always do). In most cases, they will also be disobeying orders from on high and leaving themselves open to be court-martialled (but they never are). Of course, suicide missions are always performed on a volunteer-only basis. Once, just once, it would be nice if they could find a single regular character who had enough respect for his superiors or a large enough instinct for self-preservation to turn one down.

SUSPERIA: The late Caretaker's mate. Janeway hoped the alien would use her powers to help get them home. Yeah, like someone named after a horror movie was going to be trustworthy.

SYBOK: Hitherto unmentioned half brother who slipped effortlessly into Spock's family tree in a vain attempt to make *The Final Frontier* a bit more interesting. He died before anyone could question the character's failure to come to light before this. But at least he had a proper Vulcan name.

T

T: Captain James Kirk's middle initial, which he always seemed a bit overly fond of using. Perhaps he picked it himself, some time after the revelation – in 'Where No Man Has Gone Before' – that his middle name began with an R. Now, of course, we all know that the T stands for Tiberius: Gene Roddenberry was still warm in his grave when *Star Trek VI* blatantly picked up and 'legitimised' this vital continuity point from . . . *THE ANIMATED SERIES*.

TAL SHAYA: Neck-snapping Vulcan form of execution considered merciful – wonder what the cruel methods were like? This is not to be confused in any way, shape or form with Tal Shiar, the Romulan's answer to the CIA, even though they sound exactly the same (and may well be spelt the same too, but as we haven't got access to the original scripts we'll give 'em the benefit of the doubt).

TECHNOBABBLE: A term coined by Trekkies which refers, rather over-fondly we feel, to those parts of the show which we prefer to call 'the complete and total bollocks bits'. You know the sort of thing we mean: the ship/station is at the mercy of some grotesque and powerful man with a lump on his forehead, when suddenly Scotty/cartoon Scotty/Geordi/O'Brien/Torres gets onto the old intercom and announces that they've thought of a brilliant new, never-before-imagined, completely incomprehensible scheme to get them out of this mess. No doubt it will have something to do with the phase transition coils or the warp plasma relays, or perhaps it'll involve the creation of some tetrion emissions or a tachyon funnel. It's some comfort to know, though, that a technical adviser (currently Michael Okuda) is employed to make sure that, when the characters must talk such unmitigated crap, they can at least do so with consistency. But isn't this just giving the writers an excuse to be lazy? Apparently, they're all prone to sticking [TECH] in their scripts in the sure knowledge that Okuda will fill in the gaps for them. This leads us to suspect that some unscrupulous hacks have taken advantage of the system, and that many of their manuscripts conclude thus:

> *Picard*: 'Oh no, we're being sucked into a black hole, Q is about to carry out his threat to destroy us all and the entire crew is on the verge of dying from a lethal virus, except for Doctor Crusher and myself as usual. Oh mèrde, mèrde, mèrde. What on earth can we do?'
> *Geordi*: 'I've had an idea, Captain. Why don't we just [*TECH*]?'
> [AND THEY DO.]
> *Picard*: 'Phew, that was a close one, wasn't it?'

TECHNOLOGY, 23RD- AND 24TH-CENTURY: It's not that we doubt any of *Star Trek*'s speculations about technological advancement in the next few centuries, but it would be nice if someone in the future would jump into their warp-powered ship, slingshot back in time and beam down to confirm it.

TELLARITES: Compared to those little blokes wearing fezzes and the women with big hair, simply having piggy noses stuck on their faces made this species the most convincingly alien of all the delegates in the 'Journey to Babel'.

***TEXTUAL POACHERS*:** Henry Jenkins' fascinating and long-overdue (it was published in 1992) account of the activities of television fans, which uses Trekkies as its focus. Jenkins discusses the theory that the hegemony of the ruling classes is both disseminated and propagated by media messages; however, he dismisses the view – often implied in cultural studies – that all viewers are passive receptors of these messages, and praises the approach taken by fans who not only debate the messages critically but who often re-fashion them into their own frameworks via fanzines, fiction, etc. The 'anorak' myth is thus dispelled and the intelligence and creativity of most *Star Trek* devotees is asserted. Or is it just an amusing attempt to claim that those pathetic saddoes, whose idea of stimulation is to write a story in which two *Star Trek* characters cop off, are actually well-balanced? Take your pick.

TEN TRIED AND TRUSTED WAYS OF BRINGING *STAR TREK* FANDOM INTO DISREPUTE

1: Expose your tragic fantasies by writing a piece of fan fiction – or even poetry – in which two or more of your favourite characters get down to it. Data and Tasha is a good choice, and has the added bonus that you'll be able to do one of those interminably dull pieces set between the scenes of a transmitted episode. Picard and Bev might fulfil a few wish-dreams for you, but, for ideal results, just follow the pack and get Kirk and Spock bonking. Come on, you know it's the nearest thing to real sex you'll get.

2: And, while you're giving your creative talent full leash, put lips to microphone, record your own *Star Trek* song and release it on tape so that literally ones of people can hear it and snigger at you. Practitioners of this dire art call it filk music, which is a hilarious play on the term 'folk music' (we assume).

3: Get married at a convention. You can dress up in Starfleet uniform and exchange communicators or something. When the bride arrives to the strains of the *Next Generation/Motion Picture* theme, you know you'll have brought shame upon serious fans every-where.

4: Send a series of death threats to Malcolm McDowell, the talented British character actor who, in your eyes, MURDERED THE GREATEST STARFLEET

CAPTAIN WHO EVER LIVED AND MUST PAY FOR IT WITH HIS WORTHLESS LIFE!!!

5: Take your cue from a throwaway line in *The Next Generation*, translate Hamlet into Klingonese and sell the results in public places. Fans all over the world will never live that one down.

6: Or, on a more personal level, you could allow a national newspaper to interview you about your hobby and ensure that the article hinges on your love for the Klingon language (which you sometimes use, inadvertently, in public places). If you really, really want to make a fool of yourself, you might even tell them that you don't have a girlfriend yet as you're looking for one who can whisper sweet Klingon nothings into your Spock-ears.

7: Report for jury service in full captain's regalia because you think it will make you look all respectable and official. Not only will you be immediately discharged, but you can bring further disgrace upon yourself by complaining to the papers.

8: Start a letter-writing campaign. Go on, there hasn't been one for a few days. It doesn't have to be about anything serious like the series being cancelled or bits missing from *The Motion Picture* or anything – you could go for something totally frivolous like making sure that Janeway doesn't sleep with Q, if you like. The possibilities are truly endless.

9: Go on TV's *Mastermind* answering questions on *TOS* (or *OS* as they called it) and lose, having mistaken 'The Cage' for 'Where No Man Has Gone Before'. All the more embarrassing when you're reminded that *Doctor Who* fan Gavin Fuller went on to win an earlier series.

10: Dress up as a Klingon and appear on access TV performing your own lament for the cancelled *Next Generation* ('Where did you boldly go?'). Actually, the guy who did this was probably taking the mick, and it was quite funny so we'll let him off. He should be careful though, lest he attract death threats from Trekkies who feel he is poking fun at them. Assuming they get the joke, that is.

'THANK YOU VERY MUCH. WE HAVE ONE OF OUR OWN THAT WE LIKE BETTER': Reportedly what CBS officials said to Gene Roddenberry when he presented them with his ideas for *Star Trek*. To add insult to injury, the one they liked better was *Lost in Space*.*

* And with this show as the only comparable competition on US TV in the '60s, it's not so surprising that Star Trek *garnered such an appreciative following.*

THIRD ROCK FROM THE SUN: A science fiction series you can laugh at – so plenty in common with *Star Trek* then. In one episode, George Takei appeared as himself at a *Star Trek* convention; not quite another outing for Captain Sulu, but, hell, you've got to Takei what you can get. This was probably a step up from the US sitcom *Brotherly Love*, in which George played a *Star Trek* fan so devoted that he had had his features surgically altered to resemble those of George Takei. But Jonathan Frakes went one better by almost portraying himself as an actor in a science fiction series, in *Cybill*. By 'almost' we're not suggesting that Frakes isn't a proper actor or anything (heaven forfend), it's just that nobody was allowed to say the series was *Star Trek* and his 'Starfleet' uniform was subtly different. Copyright laws eh, who needs 'em?

TIES: A range of these, with various *Star Trek* designs, are available from Ralph Marlin. But when would you wear one? On what sort of occasion is a tie necessary and yet one of these ties acceptable? Certainly not at work, if you don't want to 'come out' as a saddo to your colleagues or scare off customers. For interviews then? Yeah, like prospective employers are going to trust someone who'd spend thirteen quid on emblazoning Spock or numerous Starfleet logos across their front. At conventions, maybe – but it hardly goes with a Starfleet uniform or a Klingon costume, does it? And just going out in one is a definite no-no, unless you want to be incapable of scoring or getting into a decent club for the night, or you fancy being beaten up by bouncers for being an obvious twat. That leaves only the possibility of dressing up to meet other *Star Trek* fans, so you can sit around and admire each other's patterns at length. So, well worth the cash then.

T'ONG: Tastefully named Klingon ship in the *TNG* episode 'The Emissary'. Presumably this was a lame attempt at Klingon innuendo, as in: 'Back off or we'll ram this *T'Ong* down your throat!' or 'You're gonna get a good licking!', etc.

'TOO CEREBRAL': Criticism (sic) levelled against the original pilot episode, 'The Cage', by network executives. Hence 'Spock's Brain'.

'TOO SHORT A SEASON': If this *Next Generation* episode had only been made a year later, it would have been in the truncated season two and we could have made a joke about its name. But it wasn't.

TOPLESS SCENES: Sadly, there were very few of these in *The Original Series* and, what's worse, those we did get featured curvy Captain Kirk and sultry Mr Spock.

T'PAU: No, not the '80s pop band fronted by leggy, ginger-maned Carol Dekker (well it is them, obviously*) but we mean that old Vulcan bird in 'Amok Time'. In the old days it was much easier to guess the sex of Vulcans just by hearing their names: T'Pau and T'Pring were definitely women, Spock, Surak and Sarek were blokes. But things got a bit confusing when Saavik appeared in the films, and not just 'cos she was portrayed by two different actresses. They could have called her T'Pot or something. Maybe her parents wanted a boy? And as for Tuvok in *Voyager*, we can only assume that he is a hermaphrodite. For that matter, shouldn't Stonn – Spock's love rival in 'Amok Time' – have been called Stonk or something?

* *Despite the name, T'Pau always claimed not to be fans of* Star Trek *at all. Yeah, right, and we suppose their lead singer wasn't named after Commodore Decker then.*

TEN VULCAN NAMES THAT WOULD HAVE SUITED STONN BETTER

1: Spack.
2: Stick.
3: Suck.
4: Sock.
5: Spank.
6: Sedrik.
7: Slick.
8: Spunk.*
9: Stink.
10: Smack.

*Bob Justman was apparently even more keen than us to see that the continuity of Vulcan appellations was maintained: he believed male names should begin with 'Sp' and end in 'k' and provided a long list of possibilities. Although not having the same meaning in the States, this one was not included.

T'PEL: Vulcan character name from *The Animated Series*, which lends credence to the above theory and just proves that *TAS* is far more deserving of canonicity than any of its successors. In homage to its illustrious predecessor, *Voyager* named Tuvok's wife after her.

TRANSPORTER ACCIDENT: Useful plot standby.

TREK: The abbreviated name by which the *Star Trek* franchise is often referred to in the titles of unauthorised books on the subject. So what's the idea behind that, then? Perhaps it's a cunning ploy on the part of publishers to stop the licensers from noticing what they've done. Like they'll be scouring bookshops for evidence of unofficial merchandise and they'll think: 'What's this? A book about *Trek*? Dunno what that is, but it's obviously not an attempt to cash in on our show, because that's called *Star Trek*.' Unauthorised though this very volume is, we've decided to risk such attention for the sake of not looking so stupid.

TREKKERS' CHOICE AWARDS: Metaphorical gongs handed out during the live 30th anniversary gala, based on votes logged on the internet. The net users were also given the chance to pick their favourite award categories which, one suspects, led to some of them just taking the piss. The 'Best Example of Ingenious Engineering' Award: well bugger us with a fish slice if that didn't go to Scotty. The 'I Went to Medical School for This?' Award: excuse us? But our favourite was the 'Infinite Diversity' Award, for Star Trek's best non-humanoid life form. Hands up everyone who can name more than one. Oh all right then, so most of you can – but that's because you're sad pedantic fans, or else you wouldn't be reading this book, would you? The Tribbles won, anyway.

TREKKIES: It's hard to credit, but *Star Trek* fans actually have the equivalent of a racial slur and this is it. It started out as a generic term referring to devotees of the series, but it was soon redefined by the media as a derogatory remark aimed at mad, sad bastards who dressed as characters from the series and hung fanatically on every word spoken in it. As near as we can tell, this definition arose because ... well, because lots of Trekkies were just like that. However, there was a backlash amongst the marginally more sensible sections of fandom, who insisted that they should be called Trekkers so as not to be confused with their anti-social counterparts in any way, shape or form. Alternatively, 'fans of *Star Trek*' is an adequate label for most people.

ARE YOU A TREKKIE?
TEN DEAD GIVEAWAYS

1: You think *Deep Space Nine* will never be a patch on *The Original Series*, although you've grown to love *The Next Generation*. *Voyager*, on the other hand, is so bad that it borders on blasphemy against the late, great Gene Roddenberry – which isn't to say that you don't watch every episode.

2: You think Kirk and Spock make a beautiful couple.

3: You spent £75 on a ticket for the première of *Generations* at the Odeon, Leicester Square, just so you could sit in the same building as the cast for a couple of hours and see the film a whole week before its release.

4: You once sent off to Franklin Mint for . . . well, for anything really. Sure, their products are well-made with good materials and you might try to claim that you wanted 'something nice' for the house – but letting people know that you've laid out 200 quid for a model of the *Enterprise* with a gold-plated navigational deflector won't really enhance your status in polite society, will it?

5: You think of *Star Trek – Concordance* as your bible and find yourself nodding in agreement at some of its more salient points on the series' contribution to religion and philosophy. You look forward to a Utopian future in which hunger and strife have been eliminated and injections don't hurt.

6: You sent off for a *TV Zone* binder, which holds sixteen issues of the publication. Not that the binders themselves are too bad, but what the hell do you think you're doing with sixteen issues of *TV Zone*?

7: Having become a fluent speaker in Klingonese, you have started to learn Klingonaase: the fan-created breakaway language based on some bits of dialogue in *The Original Series.*

8: You have every novel, factual book, comic strip and novelisation based on the series and you've actually read more than, say, a quarter of them.

9: You're still reading this.

10: People tend to steer clear of you at parties.

TREKNICHIANS: Label applied by *Star Trek* fandom to that subsection of itself which is enthralled beyond all reason by the scientific implications of the programme. Treknichians spend their time figuring out how warp engines might actually work, or what the practical repercussions of the Romulans' cloaking technology would be, with a view to being able to proclaim that the events of their favourite show really could happen. There's no denying that they are intelligent people, often physics graduates with a strong understanding of theoretical principles. The depth and complexity of their calculations is frequently beyond the abilities of laymen such as ourselves to comprehend, though we have no doubt that it is usually accurate. It is perhaps unfortunate then (for them) that, beyond the realms of fanzines and the internet, the 'Treknichian' label is mostly eschewed in favour of the less respectful but equally applicable 'nerd'.

TRELANE: What a shock it was to learn that 'The Squire of Gothos' was in fact the child of powerful aliens – we were convinced he was a real Englishman. Tally-ho!

TRIBBLE DROP: Stunt designed to celebrate 30 years of *Star Trek* and to promote 'Trials and Tribble-ations'. Vast quantities of the cute furry creatures were dropped over various US locations – though not real Tribbles obviously, not least because of the great risk to agricultural regions. Good job they weren't bringing back the Doomsday Machine, really. But, hard as it is to believe, Tribbles are not universally popular among fans, so it might have been better to use something more representative of *The Original Series* as a whole: a cascade of those ubiquitous rocks (see ROCKS) perhaps. Granted, a rock drop would have been much less safe, but think of the publicity. Or they could have done a fourth Mudd story and distributed lots of beautiful women to the ravening hordes. Kirk would definitely have approved.

TRIMBLE, JOHN AND B J O: Famous American fan couple, credited with the 1967 'Save *Star Trek*' letter campaign and thus, in our eyes, entirely responsible for season three of *The Original Series*. Thanks, guys!

TUMBLE-NOT MUGS: Merchandise version of the actual

mugs, as seen on the series itself apparently. And no doubt very much like them, though we don't recall the real ones having stuff like 'Resistance is futile' and 'Live long and prosper' written on them. Of course we could be wrong, as we don't actually recall seeing them at all anyway. They are called 'tumble-not' because they won't tip over (how do you drink out of 'em then?). According to the misleadingly titled merchandise catalogue *Sci-Fi News*, this enables them to 'boldly go where no mug has gone before', but we'd have thought the opposite was true. And anyway, ordinary mugs don't topple unless you're a right clumsy twat.

'TURNABOUT INTRUDER': The very last episode of *The Original Series* (aw, shame), but the first in which we actually see Captain Kirk enter a woman.

'TUVIX': *Voyager* episode in which Tuvok and Neelix are caught in a hideous transporter accident (see TRANS-PORTER ACCIDENT) and merged into one being. We only mention this because it's got such a stupid name (to go with the stupid plot), and because the working title 'Sym-biogenesis' was much better. But if only they'd thought of this story-line in time to merge, say, Will Riker and Wesley Crusher for an episode called 'Willy Crusher'. Oh all right then, we're just being silly; let's move on to a useful and informative list instead.

TEN RECURRING CHARACTERS WHO HAVE BEEN HONOURED WITH RARE NAME CHECKS IN EPISODE TITLES*

1: Spock, in the inimitable 'Spock's Brain'. He also holds the unique distinction of being mentioned in a movie title (*Star Trek III – The Search for Spock*, in case you hadn't worked it out). Presumably, the producers wanted to make sure we all knew he was alive, well and in the film, so that we might actually go and see it.

2: Sarek. Like father, like son.

3: Harry Mudd appeared three times and never once in an episode that didn't bear his name. After his encounters with Kirk and company, his name was, erm, mud in Federation circles.

4: Data in 'Datalore', 'Elementary, Dear Data', 'Data's Day' and 'A Fistful of Datas'. Somebody must have liked him then. The first of these also features the name of another recurring character. See if you can guess whose it is.

5: Troi in 'Ménage a Troi'. Oo-er, this sounds a bit daring for *Star Trek*, doesn't it? Still, it could have been worse. She could have just taken on Riker and Worf together in an episode called 'Troilism'.

6: Q. Bet you think we're going to subject you to loads more of our made-up Q titles now, don't you? Well tough, 'cos we've run out of them.

7: Dax, who was already a regular on *Deep Space Nine* when she starred in *Star Trek*'s least imaginative title ever: 'Dax'.

8: Quark, in 'The House of Quark'. Is it just us, or does Quark's name sound like something Donald Duck might say?

9: Bashir, in 'Our Man Bashir'. We think there's a later episode too, but we can't remember the name of it and can't be bothered to look it up. It's not been on the Beeb yet anyway (at time of writing), so you can write it in here yourself when you see it.**

10: Paris, in the *Next Generation* episode 'We'll Always Have Paris'. A bit of a misnomer really, as he hadn't been created at the time. Still, it counts.

* And no, we haven't forgotten Ensign Ro; it's just that if we put eleven people in the list, it'd ruin the whole format of the book.
** It's called 'Doctor Bashir, I Presume'. We knew all along.

TUVOK: See HEMAL (which is in *Doctor Who – The Completely Useless Encyclopedia*. Go on, buy it. You know you want to. What do you mean, you can't stand *Doctor Who*?).

TV GUIDE: Aptly named digest-sized publication from America. For the week covering the 30th anniversary, it was published with four different covers, featuring Captains Kirk, Picard, Sisko, and Janeway respectively. A brilliant idea, and what a treat for the fans; but can we ever persuade Virgin to publish one of our books with a variety of covers? In a word, no. Mentioning *TV Guide* reminds us of the time we visited that backstreet shop in Manchester, the one with a sign outside boasting the largest selection of TV magazines in the city, yet we couldn't find a single television-related publication in there. Very odd.

TWAIN, MARK; AKA CLEMENS, SAMUEL: Imagine our surprise when that bloke, Jerry Hardin, who played Mark Twain in the *TNG* episode 'Time's Arrow' turned up at the Edinburgh Festival in the very same role. Unfortunately we didn't get to see the production, but presumably the narrative featured the famous author fighting Romulans and repairing warp core breaches in between writing chapters of *The Prince and the Pauper*.

TWENTIETH CENTURY: A popular era of Earth's history, at least to judge by the number of times that Starfleet crews have visited it. Many facets of the 1900s have been freakishly recreated on brave new worlds discovered by Kirk and company. By the time of 'Miri', they were obviously so used to this happening that the pseudo-1960s setting rated only a cursory mention and they didn't feel the need to have it explained. (See also CHRONOTON PARTICLES.)

UNIFORMS IN *THE ORIGINAL SERIES*, VARIATIONS OF STARFLEET: Nowadays, presumably at the insistence of the toy manufacturers, Starfleet personnel are changing their cossies all the time. But in the old days they all pretty much stuck to the same outfits, with one or two notable exceptions. Firstly, there was the green shirt worn by Kirk. And, of course, the other green shirt worn by Kirk. Then there were the dress uniforms which were pretty much like the ordinary ones, only shiny and with flashier badges on. But more importantly, there was the mustard-coloured shirt with the ribbed collar, worn by Spock in 'Where No Man Has Gone Before'. Because this episode was originally broadcast third in sequence, we feel that this top undermines the credibility of the entire series and brings *Star Trek*'s continuity crashing down around its pointed ears. Though it did kind of suit Spock, don't you think?

UNIT 3947: If they put their minds to it, the *Voyager* mob could have a profitable sideline as scrap metal merchants. One time they found that old truck floating in space, another time it was this crap robot. The fact that it looked a lot like Kamelion from *Doctor Who* wasn't enough to deter them from reactivating it, which they achieved using a convincing stream of technobabble.

UNIVERSAL TRANSLATORS: We've no idea how these things work. Captain Kirk had a go at explaining it once but we couldn't understand a bloody word he said. They tend to keep quiet about them most of the time, anyway, because they're just so stupid. So Starfleet have developed a tiny device which not only instantaneously interprets every language spoken in the vicinity, but can also redirect sound waves in such a way that the original words are no longer audible but everyone present can hear a translation in their own tongue, have they? Just the thing for chatting to sentient rocks, electric blobs, etc. Oh, but when Worf or someone actually wants to use a Klingon phrase for effect, it's allowed through. Hmmm. We're not about to complain, though, as every other SF series ever has had the same problem and who wants subtitles? So long as they keep those shows coming in Federation Standard,* we're happy.

* *Which is English, obviously.*

UPENDA: Uhura's first name, according to what was once the definitive *Star Trek* factual book, *The Officer's Manual*, though no one else has ever used it. We're not surprised; in fact, we only mention it because we find it vaguely amusing in a juvenile sort of way. Likewise, the *Manual* gave Spock's Vulcan name – never revealed in the episodes as it was considered unpronounceable by humans – as Xtmprszntwlfd. Yep, that's unpronounceable all right. Nowadays, of course, to christen your offspring thus would be regarded as child abuse (Paula Yates, take note).

VENTRILOQUISM: Kirk displayed a remarkable talent for this at the start of 'The Cloud Minders' when he managed to get out an entire sentence ('Who are you, what is the meaning of this attack?') without moving his lips.

'VOYAGE OF DISCOVERY': For fans of any SF series, the pinnacle of UK merchandising during the '70s was likely to be a set of annuals from the Manchester-based World Distributors. *Star Trek* was no exception, although its volumes disappointed by running cheap reprints of the American Gold Key strips (see X-MEN). Not to worry, there were still plenty of simplistic board games to be laughed at, and lots of World's trademarked 'Fascinating Facts Which Have Sod All To Do With The Subject Of This Book' pages. 'Voyage of Discovery' was one of these board games, appearing in the 1970 *Star Trek Annual* and perplexing readers with its unintentionally blank instruction squares. Such a novelty is no flipping use to modern-day collectors, though. For them, it's all but impossible to find a copy in which some bastard kid hasn't scrawled 'GO BAKE TO START' or 'CLINGONS ATACK – MISS 2 TURNS' to complete the publisher's job for them. However, it's well worth the effort, as this was the year when World kindly reprinted Starfleet's 'Suitability Probe' (perhaps in a bold attempt to sue the organisation for plagiarism when they write it themselves in 300 years' time). The questions themselves seem a bit simplistic but, as the starships of the future can all but fly themselves, perhaps you really can get by with just a basic knowledge of which planets are the largest and smallest in our solar system and which one has rings.

TEN NOTABLE *STAR TREK* GAMES

1: *'Star Trek:* The Role Playing Game'. The worst thing about this is that it includes lots more dull statistics about 24th-century technology, as if there weren't enough already. Hence, more fuel for Treknichians and for the internet *Star Wars* debate (see INTERNET).

2: 'Trivial Pursuit: *Star Trek* Edition'. Including some clips from episodes that you must already have seen to stand a chance of answering the questions. Their demographic sampling of fans was a bit off too, hence the back-of-box advertisement for Triv's 'family edition'.

3: *Jeu de Star Trek* Game. Simplistic 1974 board game, which deserves a mention only because the box (on which a badly drawn crew run through space) clearly marks it down as a *TAS* tie-in, and not because the title's in some bloody foreign language. Dunno what '*jeu de*' means, but we'd take a stab that 'game' means, erm, game.

4: *Star Trek*. On the other hand, this equally simplistic Palitoy creation gets a slot because it's British. According to *Star Trek Collectibles*, it's worth up to $100 in the States, but over here you can get it for 50p in most car boot sales.

5: *'Star Trek: The Next Generation – A Final Unity'*. There are hundreds of computer games, so we thought we'd better list one. And if you're struggling with it, then help is at hand in the form of a nifty cheats book. OK, so it costs 20 quid, but then they have thoughtfully stuck in an episode guide on the off-chance that you don't already own one.

6: For far less dosh, you can download the rules to three-dimensional chess – as played by Spock – from the internet. Sadly, the silver and gold playing board comes from Franklin Mint at a cost of £145.

7: 'How to Host a Murder'. Usually, the games in this series require you to take on the role of a suspect in a murder mystery. In the *Star Trek: The Next Generation* version, though, you play various crew members. So it's pretty clear that none of you dunnit, innit?

8: 'A Klingon Challenge'. Not just a bog-standard board game, this comes complete with a specially recorded video cassette on which a snarling, pastry-headed Klingon offers . . . well, a challenge, we suppose. Once that's over, you can get on with moving the counters around the board.

9: Captain Kirk pinball game. We've saved the best till almost last. In this mid '70s triumph from Azrack Hamway, the object is to get your balls into as many holes as possible. But that's not the game's only connection with Captain Kirk; no, there's also a picture of him on it. There's a Spock version too, but that's much less logical.

10: 'Starfleet Battles'. This complex strategy game (from Task Force Games) could keep you engrossed for many months, and that's just learning the rules. If anyone works out how to play it, please drop us a line and let us know. On second thoughts, don't.

VOYAGER: Federation starship which bears an uncanny resemblance to a toilet bowl, though CIC must like it as they didn't put much else on their video covers for two seasons. What a great name it has too, and what remarkable foresight on the part of whoever christened it. How could they have known it would end up going on a long voyage? Spooky!

VULCAN VILLAGE: Imagine our surprise to find that the North-West boasts such a location. We haven't been, but we can just imagine what it's like. No doubt tons of Trekkies have pitched tents there and gather on the village green each day to sing songs about *Star Trek* and burble on about Infinite Diversity in Infinite Combinations and all that tosh. Sort of a

211

UK spiritual home for them really, though there are one or two other options.

TEN GOOD PLACES FOR TREKKIES TO SETTLE IN THE UK

1: Kirk. Or, if you want to be a bit more cruel, Kirkham. Or Wigtown.

2: Worfield.

3: Bo'ness.

4: Rodden, or its 'twin' town, Bury.

5: Beverley.

6: Chapel, or even Chapeltown. There are plenty of both, as well there may be.

7: Crosby. Or, on similar lines, Burton or Dorn. All good places to raise the next generation.

8: Babel. Worth taking a journey to, don't you think?

9: Yarmouth. A place of which Data has fond memories.

10: We don't know how they're going to write out Jennifer Lien yet, so we'll throw Kesgrave into the list on the (very small) off-chance that it becomes appropriate. If not, may we suggest instead that Wesley lovers might like to try the beautiful Shetland town of Twatt.

'WAGON TRAIN TO THE STARS, A': How *Star Trek* was originally described; the *Enterprise* crew being the pioneering frontiersmen with, presumably, the Klingons representing the Indians. To be honest, it's not an entirely accurate analogy: for a start there's only one *Enterprise*, so it would have quite a job forming itself into a circle when under attack from its enemies. And we can imagine where real-life so-called pioneering frontiersmen would have shoved the Prime Directive.

WALKING BEAR, ENSIGN: Native American *Enterprise* crewmember in an episode of *The Animated Series*. Yet another example, if one were needed, of this inspirational show paving the way for its imitators . . . we're thinking in particular of *Voyager*'s derivative Chakotay.

WANG, GARRET: This *Voyager* actor had the honour of being in *People Magazine*'s list of the 50 most beautiful people. Well done mate, but in all honesty we have to say that you don't do much for us. But then neither does William Shatner, so perhaps our standards are a bit too high.

WARP FIVE: Speed to which all starships were limited when it was discovered (in *TNG*'s 'Force of Nature') that their warp drives were causing irreparable damage to the fabric of the cosmos. In practice, this made no difference to story-lines whatsoever. However, the various captains couldn't look half as macho sticking to old ladies' speeds –

and *Voyager* would have no chance of getting home – so the idea was quickly and quietly dropped.

WARP TEN: Infinite velocity or, as Neelix puts it, 'very fast'. Crossing this maximum warp threshold had eluded the greatest minds in Starfleet for decades and has been dismissed as a theoretical impossibility – which is no doubt why it took Torres, Paris and Kim a whole month to crack it. (See COCHRANE.)

WATAUGA, TEXAS: Location of the First Church of Shatnerology where founder and Archbishop John Hattan, along with 1,000 or so devotees of 'the one true Shatner', gather to worship the 'Benevolent Being' and be 'transfixed by his magnificent toupee'. There's nothing more to be said really is there?

'WAY OF THE WARRIOR': We weren't quite sure about *DS9*'s season four opener to start with. On the plus side, it had Kira and Dax in skimpy swimsuits, while going against it was the introduction to the series of that bundle of fun, Worf (with the promise of lots of slapstick comedy escapades to come in the future, we don't think). However, as the episode progressed, the tide turned very much in its favour, what with the Klingons restored to their rightful status in the *Star Trek* universe as complete bastards, which in turn gave the *DS9/Defiant* mob the opportunity to do some serious ass kicking. You just can't beat a bit of gratuitous violence, can you?

'WE'RE GOING DOWN, CAPTAIN': Line of dialogue from 'Return of the Archons', though as it was uttered by that consummate professional Mr Scott, you can be certain he was referring to his beloved *Enterprise* and not oral sex at all. Still, we've been a bit sparing with the *double entendres* so far and thought we'd better take this last opportunity to give you one.*

* *'I congratulate you on your instrumentation' is another one. Mea 3, a blonde inhabitant of Emaniar VII greeted Kirk with this line as soon as he beamed down. Blimey, if that's not a come on we don't know what is.*

'WHERE NO MAN HAS GONE BEFORE': *Star Trek* has had more pilots than British Airways. This was the second one for *The Original Series* (and, in fact, there are even two versions of this one). Even so, it still wasn't right. Radical revisions for the series proper included trimming Spock's eyebrows, dropping the untrendy ribbed collars, and changing Kirk's middle initial from R to T. They also brought on board Doctor McCoy. Given all this, it was a bit of a mistake to show the episode third in sequence. (See also UNIFORMS IN *THE ORIGINAL SERIES*, VARIATIONS OF STARFLEET.)

'WHERE NO ONE HAS GONE BEFORE': Greed and hunger may have been eliminated in Gene Roddenberry's Utopian future, but they haven't managed to get rid of political correctness yet.

WHITE RABBIT, GIANT: *Alice in Wonderland*-inspired character encountered by the original *Enterprise* crew whilst having a spot of shore leave. As *Star Trek* creatures go it wasn't on a par with the Gorn, but we reckon it'd be more than a match for the Klingons.

'WHO MOURNS FOR ADONAIS?': *TOS* episode so good it deserves a big hand.

WINN, KAI: Flippin' 'eck, is she a bitch or what? Take the *DS9* episode 'Shakaar': it started off as an everyday tale of simple Bajoran farming folk, then that venomous old bag stuck her oar in and it nearly turned into a civil war. What a cow!

WINSTON, JOHN: Unsung *TOS* stalwart, who played Transporter Chief Kyle in no less than eleven episodes, not to mention *The Wrath of Khan* (and we definitely won't mention Kyle's *Animated Series* outing, as we shouldn't be at all surprised if he was played in it by Majel Barrett). Kyle's British too! Give the man a spin-off series. (See also IN VINO VERITAS.)

TEN OTHER POTENTIAL *STAR TREK* SPIN OFFS*

1: *Star Trek: The Actual Next Generation.* A mini-series featuring the adventures of Captain Harriman as he oversees the construction of the *Enterprise B*. Guest starring William Shatner as an over-the-hill, power-mad Starfleet captain intent on wresting control of the new ship.

2: *Star Trek: The Actual Next Generation But One.* Another mini-series, this time set on the *Enterprise C*.

3: *Star Trek: The Next Penetration.* A more tasteful version of the porn classic. Starring Denise Crosby, Marina Sirtis, Michelle Forbes, Nana Visitor, Terry Farrell, Chase Masterson, Jennifer Lien and Roxann (Biggs-)Dawson. Plus the return of former *Star Trek* guest stars Teri Hatcher, Madchen Amick, Famke Janssen, Ashley Judd . . . What do you mean, 'wishful thinking'?

4: *Star Trek Kids.* The youthful antics of Little Jimmy Kirk, Master Spock, Bones and Wee Scotty. We know it sounds naff, but, after all, they considered doing a film along similar lines (see *FIRST ADVENTURE, THE*).

5: *Star Trek: The Next Generation – The Animated Series.*** The original cast provide their own voices; Majel Barrett does the rest.

6: *Star Trek: The Live-Action Series.* The further adventures of Lieutenant Arex and M'Ress following their posting from the *Enterprise*.

7: *Star Trek Team-Up.* Following the success of the X-Men comic book crossover (see X-MEN), various popular TV characters turn up in space: Al Bundy, Frasier, Xena: Warrior Princess, Mad Murdoch off The A-Team . . . Oh, have they?

8: *Star Trek: DSV.* Series set on an underwater version of the *Enterprise*. Admittedly, this one's more than likely to sink without trace, but it would provide the perfect excuse to reintroduce the aquashuttle from *The Animated Series*.

9: *Captain Sulu and the Excelsior.* No, on second thoughts, that sounds a bit crap.

10: *Star Trek: The Last Generation.* Futuristic exploits aboard the *Enterprise Z.*

* And we have absolutely no intention of including what seems to be the current favourite among the internet community, Star Trek: The Original Series season four, to be achieved using either 'Trials and Tribble-ations'-esque computer stuff, a 24th-century setting (as half of them are there already) or lots of make-up. The original cast back together on TV? Fat chance!
** Something along these lines was actually mooted recently, but the idea was rejected as it would apparently 'cheapen the franchise'. Hmm, we thought that was what Voyager was for.

WOOLLY HAT: Entirely convincing item of disguise that enables Spock to wander freely around 20th-century Earth passing for a badly dressed human. Convincing disguise, that is until someone pulls the bugger off (the hat we mean).

WORF: Character whose dalliances with Deanna Troi and Dax would seem to disprove that old chestnut about women falling for men with a sense of humour. But why, oh why, oh why didn't Playmates release a space-suited Worf figure from *First Contact*? How are we supposed to re-enact this significant *Star Trek* adventure without it? It wouldn't be so bad if Worf's appearance at this juncture wasn't crucial in defeating the Borg. And it's not as if the toy firm are averse to making Worf figures, is it?

TEN WORF FIGURES

1: Worf as Starfleet Academy cadet. Ahh, doesn't he look sweet.
2: Wearing his original *Enterprise D* uniform, the one he wore before Tasha Yar's convenient death allowed him to take over security.
3: Pretending to be dead hard in Klingon battledress.

4: Looking cool in the black 'Rescue' outfit.

5: Looking like a twat in cowboy get-up from 'A Fistful of Datas'.

6: Governor Worf from 'All Good Things'.

7: In ritual attire for, er, conducting rituals in.

8: As a sailor from *Generations*.

9: In an unused *Generations* uniform. So what the bloody hell's the point then? Typical, they can do this, which is no use whatsoever for recreating exciting adventures, and yet they neglect to do the crucial *First Contact* spacesuit.

10: *First Contact* uniform. Yes, yes, but it's no good is it, because you can only get half-way through the film, so why bother at all?

WORLD WAR III: Gene Roddenberry's Utopian portrayal of humanity's future suffered a bit of a knock when *The Next Generation* revealed that we'd have to survive this nuclear conflict in order to reach it – and more so when *First Contact* dated it to the 2050s, during some of our lifetimes. That's quite apart from various Galactic Wars, the Eugenics War* and the flooding of the planet with ultra-violet radiation due to the depletion of the ozone layer, which is to occur in the 21st century too. So most of us are going to be wiped out. Great! Do they think we're even remotely comforted by the prospect of a few good times afterwards?

* Dunno what that was, but apparently it's already happened and we didn't notice, so perhaps it wasn't so bad after all.

WRITERS' STRIKE: Industrial action taken by the American Writers' Guild, which had a dreadful effect upon season two of *The Next Generation*. Not only did it lose four episodes – even after using a recycled script from *Star Trek II* – but its series première was delayed and its finale, 'Shades of Gray', was left without a plot at all.

X

XANDER IN LOST UNIVERSE, GENE RODDEN-BERRY'S: Described by publishers Techno Comix as 'the final legacy of legendary *Star Trek* creator Gene Roddenberry' so, of course, it's about hugely over-endowed, scantily clad women in a science fiction setting. It began with issue 0, perhaps in a bold attempt to be cancelled before issue 1, which it didn't quite manage. Another slightly longer-lived title from the same company was *Leonard Nimoy's Primortals*, which Nimoy co-created with Isaac Asimov (for someone else to write, as with *Xander*). It stepped on the toes of the eighth *Star Trek* film somewhat by chronicling man's first contact with an alien race – and no, it wasn't the Vulcans, though that would be a logical assumption.

X-MEN: *Star Trek* doesn't really work in comic strip form, but this hasn't stopped everyone and his dog from trying it. Most recently, Marvel set up the Paramount Comics label to cash in on their new parent company's characters. In practice, this meant one comic based on *Mission: Impossible* and thousands based on *Star Trek*. Alas, they quickly applied their usual policy of letting good writing and artwork take a back seat to naff crossovers; thus Marvel's over-hyped team of mutant misfits paid an inappropriate and unwelcome call on the *Enterprise* crew in a one-off special titled 'Star Trex' and advertised as 'the team-up . . . to beam up'. Hmmm. Seems to us the whole thing was orchestrated just for the sake of the panel in which someone shouts 'Doctor McCoy' across a crowded room and both Bones and the X-Men's Beast (an earlier fictional Doctor McCoy) turn around. If so, we're amazed at the writer's restraint – considering that Marvel's UK branch publishes *Doctor Who* – in not throwing the seventh Doctor in there too. At the time of writing (*Star Trek* comics are notoriously prone to cancellation), Marvel are publishing five titles, including the rather novel (for about two issues) *Early Voyages*, which features Captain Pike and co. They're also doing *Voyager*, the first issue of which boasted that the stranded crew were 'appearing for the first time ever in their own comic book series'. Gosh! And there's an X-Men/*Next Generation* crossover in the offing. We can hardly wait.

TEN MORE SPIN-OFF COMIC BOOK SERIES

1: *Star Trek* (Gold Key). The first nine had photo covers, which apparently means that dealers can charge what the hell they like for them, don't ask us why. The *Comic Book Price Guide* gives issue 1 (1967) a value, in near-mint condition, of $450 or £300, so it's probably worth at least half that much. It was so successful that issue 2 hit the stands a mere eleven months later.

2: *TV 21*. Alas, not the glossy full-colour photo-gravure broadsheet, which featured beautifully drawn adventures of the best series from the Gerry Anderson stable, but the cheap and tacky follow-up which also had Joe 90 in it.

3: *TV Comic*. For those of you who aren't aware of it, this children's publication ran in the UK from the 1950s to the 1980s. Along the way, it featured many puppet, cartoon and live-action characters from television: well-loved creations like Muffin the Mule (now sadly illegal), Popeye and Doctor Who. *Star Trek* too featured for a while, and these home-grown exploits proved almost as exciting as those of Basil Brush.

4: *Star Trek* (Marvel). Yes, they had the rights once before, in the wake of the first film, er, motion picture (they started by adapting it). Sadly for them, they were forced to cancel the book after eighteen issues, having accidentally filled it with crap.

5: *Future Tense* (Marvel UK). Reprints of the American series were right at home in this black-and-white weekly, alongside such great science fiction characters as the Micronauts, Rom – Spaceknight and, erm, Conan the Barbarian.

6: *Star Trek* (DC). In fact they did two series, having renumbered – after another eleven-month gap – in 1989. They also put out a few specials, including adaptations of the movies from III onwards (so what about II, then?), and they got Walter Koenig to do a bit of scripting (after his writing success on *The Animated Series*) in a bold but doomed attempt to sell some copies.

7: *Star Trek: The Next Generation* (DC). There was more than one of these too: their six-issue mini-series was successful, so they launched an ongoing monthly at the same time as their second *Star Trek* book and several mini-series and specials thereafter. John de Lancie wrote a few. The print version of Will Riker had a washboard stomach.

8: *Star Trek* (Marvel UK). They'd given up on their own material by now – so, in an unprecedented move, they reprinted DC's stuff (and some Starlog articles) for a British audience. Didn't work, though.

9: *Star Trek: Deep Space Nine* (Malibu). Another two ongoing series in fact (plus assorted minis, specials, blah, blah). Volume 2 was launched in 1996 to coincide with Marvel's *Deep Space Nine* comic, presumably to stuff up its sales or at least to benefit from them. As far as we're aware, this was the first time two companies have had the same title ongoing simultaneously (though Malibu's didn't last long). For another novelty, check out *Star Trek: Deep Space Nine/The Next Generation* and *Star Trek: The Next Generation/Deep Space Nine* from Malibu and DC respectively. The complexities of inter-company crossovers meant that this four-part story was split between two two-issue books with different titles, writers and publishers, and independent numbering but the same logo. Makes sense to us.

10: *The Official Star Trek Monthly* (Titan): They too

began by including US comic strip reprint material (DC stuff, if we remember rightly), but later dropped it in favour of material people actually wanted to read.

———◆———

XON: Vulcan character as almost played by David Gautreaux. He was supposed to be the *Enterprise*'s science officer in the never-made *Star Trek II*, because Leonard Nimoy said, 'I am not Spock' and declined to take part in the project. But then the TV series idea evolved into a multi-million dollar movie and Nimoy for some reason had a change of heart and said, 'You bet I'm Spock!' So Xon became the Vulcan who never was – a good thing too with a name like that – and, by way of compensation, Gautreaux got to play the small role of Commander Branch in *The Motion Picture*. Not ideal perhaps, but at least they didn't add insult to injury by offering him the part of Lt. Sonak, another ill-fated Vulcan science officer, who nearly made it aboard the *Enterprise* but was killed in a freak transporter accident. Or maybe they did offer it and he told them where to shove it.

Y

YANGS: Bitter enemies of the Kohms in the less-than-subtle allegory that was 'The Omega Glory'.

'YOU DON'T HAVE TO IMPRESS ME WITH YOUR TECHNOBABBLE': Words of wisdom from Neelix, which alas went unheeded. (See TECHNOBABBLE.)

'YOU PEOPLE ARE UNDER THE MISTAKEN IMPRESSION THAT I MAKE *STAR TREK* FOR YOU. I MAKE *STAR TREK* FOR ME!': Gene Roddenberry's infamous retort when, at a convention in Los Angeles, he was heckled by the audience for his decision to write Beverly Crusher out of *The Next Generation*. Interesting, that.

'YOU SILLY CULTS': Typical headline from the *Daily Star* relating to a feature about a controversial poll of cult TV shows in which (shock! horror!) *Star Trek* came top, beating *The X Files* into second place. Not surprisingly, fans of the latter show feared a conspiracy had taken place. Paranoia maybe, but their argument that all four *Star Trek* series had been counted as one was sound up to a point. What they failed to take into account was the likelihood that no bugger would have voted for *Voyager* – in fact that series could have lost *Star Trek* points. Another thing the *Star* neglected to mention was who actually conducted this poll of the 50 top cult shows anyway? We'd certainly never heard of it, which perhaps explains the absence of *Prisoner: Cell Block H* from the list.

Z

ZIMMERMAN, DOCTOR: Not the name of Robert Picardo's holographic character in *Voyager* (though it was considered at an early stage), despite its use by fans who seem unable to accept that a computer program wouldn't have a name. He is listed simply as 'The Doctor' in the credits, which seems to us to be a bit of a cynical attempt to cash in on the success of *Doctor Who*. It was a bit much when he (or someone much like him) appeared in *First Contact* too and was attacked by the Cybermen-like Borg. Just like watching a missing episode of the veteran series, in fact.

◆

TEN MORE THINGS THAT *STAR TREK* HAS IN COMMON WITH *DOCTOR WHO*

1: For years a heated debate raged over which series used the planet Vulcan first, though a quick look at the broadcast dates would have revealed that it was *Star Trek*. Fortunately, the original notion of having Mr Spock hail from Mars was dropped – everyone knows it's the Ice Warriors who come from Mars.

2: No arguments about who appeared first in the *Mighty Midget* Comics given away free with *Mighty TV Comic*. Issue 1 featured *Doctor Who*, issue 2 had *Star Trek*. So there.

3: Both series had stories entitled 'The Chase'. The *TNG* episode explained why most alien races in *Star Trek* are humanoid with bumps on their heads, while the six-part *Doctor Who* adventure was notable for featuring Peter Purves as Morton Dill.

4: The first of Dax's hosts (the one that looked like Nana Visitor) was apparently called Leela – and the Doctor travelled with a scantily clad savage called Leela for a couple of years. Amazing or what?

5: In *DS9* Daphne Ashbrook played the eponymous Melora. At one point the intention was to feature the gravitationally challenged Melora as a regular, but logistical reasons made this too impractical. In the Universal version of *Doctor Who*, Daphne Ashbrook portrayed the Doctor's partner Grace Holloway; again logistical reasons precluded a second outing for Dr Holloway – the movie was crap so they didn't make any more.

6: Both programmes have inspired big screen spin-off series in which the even-numbered films are far superior to the odd-numbered ones. And Leonard Nimoy was all but signed up to produce the latest mega-grossing, blockbusting *Doctor Who* movie, so you'd all have to have gone and seen that (if they'd ever bothered to make it).

7: The gunfight at the O.K. Corral formed the basis of episodes for both series. The *Star Trek* version 'Spectre of the Gun' took place on an alien world in a bizarre half town, but still managed to be as historically accurate as *Doctor Who*'s 'The Gunfighters'.

8: *Doctor Who* has had eight Doctors. And so has *Star Trek*: Dr Philip Boyce, Dr Mark Piper, Dr Leonard 'Bones' McCoy, Dr Christine Chapel, Dr Beverly Crusher, Dr Katherine Pulaski, Dr Julian Bashir and Dr Emergency Medical Holographic Program on *Voyager*. We suppose *Star Trek* fans could claim nine and include the Emergency Medical Program Doctor on the *Enterprise E*, but *Who* fans could then counter with Peter Cushing and Richard Hurndall.

9: Both series faced cancellation, refused to lie down, and returned bigger and worse than ever with a big-budget movie. But only one of them went on to have lots more movies and three spin-off series.

10: Both have lots of really sad fans, allowing books like this to sell. In fact, if you can't quite follow some of the

234

above, we suggest you pick up a copy of *Doctor Who – The Completely Useless Encyclopedia*, and all will become clear.

———◆———

Which sounds like an appropriate note on which to end.

BIBLIOGRAPHY

Not too many *Star Trek* books actually, but a surprising number ostensibly about something called *Trek*. The trouble is, most of the specialist shops put their books in sealed-up polythene bags – so how are you supposed to read 'em then?

Anyway, here's some of the stuff we found most useful:

BOOKS

Star Trek: Where No One Has Gone Before. The paperback version with both *Enterprise*s on the cover and 30 pages of extra stuff inside ... Don't tell us you forked out on one of the hardback editions.

Trek: The Unofficial A–Z. It must be good, it doesn't have an entry for Banana Split.

Star Trek Collectibles. But we're still looking for those 1990s BBC annuals that are listed.

Radio Times Official Collector's Edition: Star Trek – 30 Years.

All the *Star Trek: Voyager* novels. Nah, only joking.

MAGAZINES

Deep Space Nine Magazine, Volume 20 – the 'Women of DS9' issue.

The Official Star Trek Fact Files. Up to the point when the newsagent says, 'Hey, this isn't a library!' Sometimes sooner, if any of the loosely stuck-in pages come out and it seems prudent to make a hasty exit.

Femme Fatales, Volume 6, number 2. '*Star Trek*'s Sexiest 50'.

Star Trek Monthly. A damn fine publication, especially Gary Russell's fantastic book-review section. Come to think of it, aren't Titan doing lots of great stuff lately?

Also, some stuff from the internet, particularly the regular postings of Otto Heuer, but particularly not anything that mentioned *Star Wars*.

THE SEEMINGLY OBLIGATORY LIST OF CORRECTIONS TO THE AUTHORS' LAST WORK, WHICH ONLY LEAVES YOU TO WONDER WHY THEY COULDN'T JUST GET THEIR FACTS RIGHT IN THE FIRST PLACE

Yes, impossible though it may seem, a tiny error or two crept into *Doctor Who – The Completely Useless Encyclopedia*, giving us the opportunity to plug it again here and to make *Doctor Who* completists buy this book too. They go like this:

BANDRELL AMBASSADOR: Fortunately, no one noticed the grotesque misspelling that afflicted the word 'Bandril'. We've no excuse at all, except that the Mandrells look a bit silly too, so perhaps we were thinking of them. Like the Bandril Ambassador's operator, we put our hands up.

CAKE: Gosh, imagine our surprise when the factory in which this unique item was being baked was burnt down and it never came out after all. Similar fires at Dapol and at the Longleat Exhibition lead us to suspect an arson conspiracy, perhaps carried out by a mad *Babylon 5* fan (what other type is there?). Or maybe some incurable *Doctor Who* completist is destroying those places that bleed him of the most money for the least return. Well, we're on to your little game: we've alerted the police and the offices of Boxtree have been staked out.

K2: The name of Kettlewell's experimental robot was, of course, K1, as pointed out by Dave Owen in his *Doctor Who*

Magazine review. Blimey, that's the last time we pay you a compliment in one of our books, you ugly long-haired bastard. He was wrong about the GoGos, though.

LONDON (FICTIONAL): Some people have claimed that you didn't actually have to travel via Mars to reach the *Doctor Who* Exhibition and that it was all, in fact, a cunning illusion achieved by visual effects. Well listen maties, we were in that shuttle, we felt it buffeted by cosmic turbulence and all and, what's more, the captain himself appeared on a viewscreen and assured us that we were in fact in space. So don't try to tell us different.

WHOVIANS: Our list of alternative names for *Doctor Who* fans should have included 'Who-mosexuals'. However, someone thought this too offensive and cut it, hence this second attempt to get it into print.

And that's all the ones we're admitting to. If you've spotted any mistakes in *The Completely Useless* Star Trek *Encyclopedia* which you feel should be corrected in a subsequent volume, then you're a sad pedantic git aren't you?

INDEX